Arthur Clutton-Brock

The cathedral church of York

Description of its fabric and a brief history of the archi-episcopal see

Arthur Clutton-Brock

The cathedral church of York
Description of its fabric and a brief history of the archi-episcopal see

ISBN/EAN: 9783337259556

Printed in Europe, USA, Canada, Australia, Japan

Cover: Foto ©Lupo / pixelio.de

More available books at **www.hansebooks.com**

BELL'S CATHEDRAL SERIES:
EDITED BY GLEESON WHITE
AND EDWARD F. STRANGE

YORK

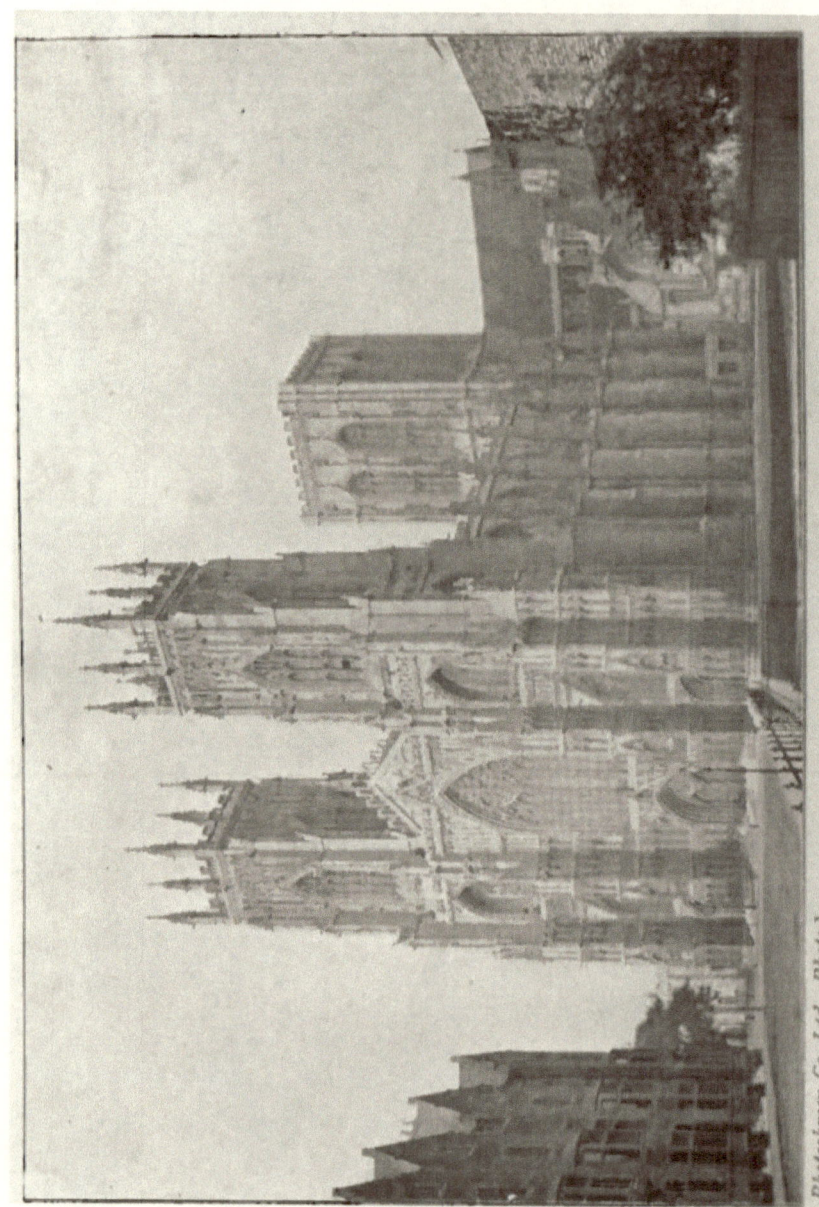

Photochrom Co. Ltd., Photo.]

YORK MINSTER, THE WEST FRONT AND NAVE.

THE CATHEDRAL CHURCH OF YORK

A DESCRIPTION OF ITS FABRIC AND A BRIEF HISTORY OF THE ARCHI-EPISCOPAL SEE

BY
A. CLUTTON-BROCK

WITH FORTY-ONE ILLUSTRATIONS

LONDON GEORGE BELL & SONS 1899

W. H. WHITE AND CO. LTD.
RIVERSIDE PRESS, EDINBURGH

GENERAL PREFACE

This series of monographs has been planned to supply visitors to the great English Cathedrals with accurate and well illustrated guide-books at a popular price. The aim of each writer has been to produce a work compiled with sufficient knowledge and scholarship to be of value to the student of Archæology and History, and yet not too technical in language for the use of an ordinary visitor or tourist.

To specify all the authorities which have been made use of in each case would be difficult and tedious in this place. But amongst the general sources of information which have been almost invariably found useful are:—(1) the great county histories, the value of which, especially in questions of genealogy and local records, is generally recognised; (2) the numerous papers by experts which appear from time to time in the Transactions of the Antiquarian and Archæological Societies; (3) the important documents made accessible in the series issued by the Master of the Rolls; (4) the well-known works of Britton and Willis on the English Cathedrals; and (5) the very excellent series of Handbooks to the Cathedrals originated by the late Mr John Murray; to which the reader may in most cases be referred for fuller detail, especially in reference to the histories of the respective sees.

GLEESON WHITE.
EDWARD F. STRANGE.

AUTHOR'S PREFACE

I HAVE usually followed Professor Willis in his account of the Minster, and my obligations to his excellent works are general and continuous.

Professor Willis made careful and extensive observations of the Crypt and other parts of the Minster during the restoration, which gave him opportunities for investigation now impossible. He also brought to these observations a learning and sagacity probably greater than those of any other writer on English Gothic Architecture, and his little book remains the standard work on the history of the Minster.

I regret that I have been unable to agree with several of the theories of that most enthusiastic and diligent writer, Mr John Browne, or even to discuss them as I should have liked; but his books must always be of great value to every one interested in the history of York. I am also indebted to Canon Raine's excellent works and compilations; to Mr Winston for his remarks on the glass in the Minster; and to Professor Freeman for his interesting criticisms of the fabric generally.

A. C.-B.

CONTENTS

	PAGE
CHAPTER I.—History of the See and City	3
CHAPTER II.—History of the Building	30
CHAPTER III.—Description of the Exterior	47
The West Front	48
The North Transept	56
The Chapter-House	60
The Choir	61
The South Transept	63
The Central Tower	67
CHAPTER IV.—Description of the Interior	68
The Nave	68
The Transepts	80
The Chapter-House	93
The Choir	98
The Crypt	120
The Record Room	123
Monuments	125
Stained Glass	133
CHAPTER V.—The Archbishops	140

ILLUSTRATIONS

	PAGE
York Minster, the West Front and Nave	*Frontispiece*
Arms of the See	*Title Page*
The Minster and Bootham Bar, from Exhibition Square	2
St Mary's Abbey	9
Bootham Bar	15
Walmgate Bar	19, 24
Micklegate Bar	25
The Shambles	29
The Minster (from an Old Print)	35
The West Front (1810)	39
The East End (from Britton)	43
The West Front—Main Entrance	49
The Exterior, from the South-East	53
The Exterior, from the North	57
Bay of Choir—Exterior	62
South Transept—Porch	65
Seal of St Mary's Abbey	67
The Nave	69
The Nave—South Aisle	77
South Transept, Triforium, and Clerestory	91
Chapter-House—Entrance and Sedilia	97
The Choir Screen	100
The Choir, looking East	101
Bay of Choir—Interior	103
The Choir, looking West	107
Compartment of Ancient Choir Stalls	110
Compartment of Altar Screen	111
The Choir in 1810	115
The Virgin and Child (a Carving behind the Altar)	119
The Crypt	121
Capitals in Crypt	122, 123
Effigy of Manley	125
Effigy of Archbishop de Grey	128
Monument of William of Hatfield	129
Monument of Archbishop Bowet	132
The East Window	138
Effigy of Archbishop Savage	151
Tomb of Archbishop Savage	152
PLAN OF MINSTER	157

Photochrom Co. Ltd., Photo.
YORK MINSTER (WEST) AND BOOTHAM BAR, FROM EXHIBITION SQUARE.

YORK MINSTER

CHAPTER I

HISTORY OF THE SEE AND CITY

AT York the city did not grow up round the cathedral as at Ely or Lincoln, for York, like Rome or Athens, is an immemorial—a prehistoric—city; though like them it has legends of its foundation. Geoffrey of Monmouth, whose knowledge of Britain before the Roman occupation is not shared by our modern historians, gives the following account of its beginning:—
"Ebraucus, son of Mempricius, the third king from Brute, did build a city north of Humber, which from his own name, he called Kaer Ebrauc—that is, the City of Ebraucus—about the time that David ruled in Judea." Thus, by tradition, as both Romulus and Ebraucus were descended from Priam, Rome and York are sister cities; and York is the older of the two. One can understand the eagerness of Drake, the historian of York, to believe the story. According to him the verity of Geoffrey's history has been excellently well vindicated, but in Drake's time romance was preferred to evidence almost as easily as in Geoffrey's, and he gives us no facts to support his belief, for the very good reason that he has none to give.

Abandoning, therefore, the account of Geoffrey of Monmouth, we are reduced to these facts and surmises. Before the Roman invasion the valley of the Ouse was in the hands of a tribe called the Brigantes, who probably had a settlement on or near the site of the present city of York. Tools of flint and bronze and vessels of clay have been found in the neighbourhood. The Brigantes, no doubt, waged intermittent war upon the neighbouring tribes, and on the wolds surrounding the city are to be found barrows and traces of fortifications to which they retired from time to time for safety. The position of York would make it a favourable one for a settlement. It stands at the head of a fertile and pleasant valley and on the banks of a tidal river. Possibly there were tribal settlements on the eastern wolds in the neighbourhood in earlier and still more barbarous times, before the Brigantes found it safe to make a permanent home in the valley, but this is all conjecture. It is not until the Roman conquest of Britain that York enters into history. The Brigantes were subdued between the years 70 and 80 A.D. by Patilius Cerealis and Agricola. The Romans called the city by the name of Eburacum. The derivation is not known. It has been suggested that it was taken from the river Ure, a tributary of the Ouse, but variations of the word are common in the Roman Empire, as, for example, Eburobriga, Eburodunum, and the Eburovices. These are probably all derived from some common Celtic word. In process of time, perhaps in the reign of the Emperor Severus—that is to say, about the beginning of the third century A.D.—the name was changed to Eboracum: from this was derived the later British name Caer Eabhroig or Ebrauc. The Anglo-Saxon name was Eoferwic, corrupted by the Danes into Jorvik or Yorvik, which by an easy change was developed into the modern name of York. In the York Museum is preserved a monument to a standard-bearer of the 9th legion, which is probably of the period of Agricola, and it is likely that Eburacum became the headquarters of the Roman army in the north soon after the conquest. It became the chief military town in the island; for, whereas the southern tribes were soon subdued, those in the north were long rebellious, and it was natural that the chief centre for troops should be established in the more disturbed parts of Britain. Close to York was the town of Isurium (Aldborough), where remains of pavements have been discovered, and where it is probable that the wealthier citizens of York had their homes. Eburacum was fortified in or before the reign of Trajan, and was connected by a system of roads with other important Roman towns. The Roman Camp lay on the east side of the river, on or near the site of the present minster. One of its corner towers and fragments of the wall still remain, and parts of the city gates have been discovered. The camp at first covered about seventy acres of ground; it was afterwards enlarged on the south. The modern streets of Petergate and Stonegate represent the roads which passed through this camp, and Bootham Bar is on the site of one of the gates. Remains of Roman pavement have been discovered below Stonegate. The city itself spread westward over the river, and fragments of houses and tesselated pavements have been discovered. In 1841 remains of public baths were found; and there are many signs that there was a large population on this side of the river. In 1854 there was found near the southern gate of the camp a tablet dedicated to Trajan, and commemorating the conclusion of some work done by the 9th legion in the year 108-9. This work was perhaps the palace of the emperors.

Near the south gate also was a Christian Church of St. Crux. The road to Tadcaster was lined with tombs, and remains of cemeteries have been discovered all round the city.

As in London, there are few remains of Roman masonry above ground, and this is but natural, for the city has been burnt and destroyed, wholly or partially, many times; and there is no doubt that Roman buildings were used, as in Rome and other cities, as a quarry for later erections.

York is historically connected with several of the emperors. Two of them, Severus and Constantius Chlorus, died there, and Constantine the Great, the son of the latter, was hailed emperor at York, if it was not the scene of his birth. At York also were the headquarters of two of the legions, the 9th and the 6th; and there is little doubt that in course of time it came to be regarded as the capital of the island. In fact, according to Professor Freeman (*Macmillan's Magazine*, Sept. 1876), "Eburacum holds a place which is unique in the history of Britain, which is shared by only one other city in the lands north of the Alps (Trier, Augusta Trevirorum)." We learn little of the history of York from Roman historians, and next to nothing of the early Christian Church. There is mention of York at rare intervals, when it became connected with the general history of the empire. For instance, in 208, Severus was in York, and it became for a time the headquarters of the court.

The Emperor Constantius died at York in 306, and there is a tradition that hundreds of years afterwards his body was found under the Church of St. Helen-on-the-Walls, with a lamp still burning over it. Many churches in the neighbourhood of Eburacum were dedicated to his wife Helena, the legendary finder of the True Cross. It has been supposed that Constantine the Great was born at York, but this is probably untrue, though he was proclaimed emperor there. In the middle of the fourth century the Picts and Scots began to make inroads, and it is probable that they captured York about 367 A.D. They were shortly afterwards driven northwards by Theodosius the Elder. At the beginning of the fifth century there were further invasions repelled by Stilicho, but in 409 the Emperor Honorius withdrew the Roman troops from Britain, and the Roman period in the history of York came to an end.

Of the early ecclesiastical history of York less even is known than of the civil. There are few relics of Roman Christianity in the city.

A stone coffin, with an apparently Christian inscription, and several Roman ornaments bearing crosses have been found and placed in the York Museum, but this is all. There is no evidence, documentary or other, of the manner in which Christianity reached York. The Christian historians give us only the most meagre references to the history of the faith in Britain. Tertullian, for example, mentions that parts of the island as yet unvisited by the Romans had been evangelised by British missionaries, and, if this were so, it would seem to prove that the Church in Britain was early active and flourishing. It is not until 314 A.D. that we come upon a definite historical fact. This was the date of the Council of Arles, convened by Constantine, to consider the Donatist Heresy, and among the bishops there assembled were three from Britain—"Eborus, Episcopus de Civitate Eboracensi; Restitutus, Episcopus de Civitate Londinensi; Adelfius, Episcopus de Civitate Col. Londinensium" (perhaps Lincoln). These bishops are mentioned in the order of precedence, and it would appear that the See of York at that time was the most important, or perhaps the oldest, in Britain. Bishops of York were also present at the Councils of Nicaea, Sardica, and Arminium. With these facts our knowledge of the Roman see of Eburacum begins and ends. The Episcopal succession probably continued for some time after the Roman evacuation, and the legendary names of Sampson, Pyramus or Pyrannus, and Theodicus have been handed down as bishops of York during the struggle with the Anglo-Saxon invaders. For a long time after the Roman evacuation jewels and plate were discovered in the neighbourhood; and in the Pontificate of Egbert, an archbishop in the eighth century, there is a special form of prayer for hallowing vessels discovered on the sites of heathen temples and houses. The great Wilfrid also, in the seventh century, speaks of recovering the sacred places from which the British clergy had been forced to flee. It is unknown when or how York was finally captured, but in the seventh century it was certainly in the hands of the English; though there still remained an independent British kingdom of Elmete, only a few miles to the west of the city. Close to York has been discovered a large burying-place of heathen Angles, in which the ashes were deposited in urns; the date of this is probably the beginning of the sixth century, and at that time the invaders must have been settled in the country, and perhaps in the city itself. The conquest marks a change in the position of York. Under the Roman occupation it had been an important city for military purposes, and for that reason it was the seat of an important bishopric. After the second conversion of England it becomes important more and more for ecclesiastical reasons, and when it plays a part in the history of England it is because of the action of its bishops; from this time, therefore, it becomes necessary to say less about the city itself and more about the see.

After the Anglo-Saxon conquest of the North of England the country between the Tweed and the Humber was divided into two kingdoms, Bernicia to the north of the Tees, and Deira to the south. In the reign of Ethelfrith these two kingdoms were united, under the name of Northumbria. Edwin, his successor, was the most powerful king in England, and every state except Kent acknowledged his supremacy.

In the troubles after the Roman evacuation, it is probable that York lost some of its importance, which it regained under Edwin, and became again the capital of England. It is at this period that the authentic ecclesiastical history of the see, and indeed of England, really begins. In 601 Gregory the Great, in a letter to Augustine, gave him authority to appoint twelve bishops in England, and among them a bishop of York, who, if his mission was prosperous, was to ordain further bishops in the North of England, remaining himself the chief of them, and being invested with the pall, the mark of a metropolitan bishop. Provision was made that the first bishop of York should be subordinate to Augustine, but that subsequently the question of seniority was to be decided by priority of consecration. Thus early did the question of precedence between York and Canterbury arise.

We may take it that the early Christian church had entirely died out in Northumbria, and that prior to the mission sent by Gregory there had been no effort in the southern part of the kingdom, at least, to reclaim the inhabitants from heathendom. York was chosen as the seat of the metropolitan bishop in the north, entirely because of its importance as a city. It is after this event that it becomes chiefly remarkable for its ecclesiastical importance. Augustine died before he had followed Gregory's instructions, and they were not carried out till 625. In that year, Justus, the fourth bishop of Canterbury, was led by unusually favourable circumstances to consecrate a bishop of York and to send him to Northumbria. Edwin the king was over-lord of England, and he wished to be allied with Kent, the only other independent kingdom in the country. He therefore proposed to marry Ethelburga, the daughter of the King of Kent. She and her father were Christians, and Edwin, though still a heathen, agreed that she should be allowed to take with her a Christian chaplain to Northumberland. Paulinus, perhaps a Briton by birth, was chosen for this office, and was consecrated Bishop of York before he set out. He has been identified with a certain Rum the son of Urien. This enterprise met with great and immediate success, in which political reasons probably played a considerable part; and on Easter-day 627, the most important date in the ecclesiastical history of York, the king Edwin, his family, and many of his court were baptised there in a wooden chapel temporarily erected on the site of the present minster. Immediately afterwards Edwin begun to build a church of stone, dedicated to St. Peter, on the same site. The baptism of the king was followed by a wholesale conversion of thousands of his subjects, and it is stated that Paulinus was forced to stay over a month in one place to baptise the crowds who flocked to him. Paulinus was confirmed in his appointment to the see by the king, and immediately after received the pall, together with Honorius of Canterbury, which authorised him to assemble councils and to consecrate bishops. The pall was not given to any of his successors until Egbert (732 A.D.). In view of the subsequent

ST. MARY'S ABBEY.

struggles for precedence between the sees of Canterbury and York, the following passage in a letter from the Pope to Edwin is of interest :—" We have ordered," the Pope says, " two palls, one for each of the metropolitans, that is for Honorius and Paulinus, that in case one of them is called from this life, the other may, in virtue of this our authority, appoint a bishop in his place." (Bede, " Eccl. Hist.," Smith edit., book ii., cap. 17, p. 98.)

This early prosperity of the northern Church did not last long. In 633 Edwin was defeated and killed at a battle near Hatfield, and a period of anarchy and persecution followed. Thereupon Paulinus, with Ethelburga, the queen, fled to Kent, leaving behind him only one evangelist, by name James the Deacon. It is probable that the greater part of Northumbria thereupon fell back into paganism, and by the flight of Paulinus the Catholic Church, or that part of it immediately under the influence and control of the bishops of Rome, lost its hold on the north, which it was not to regain without a struggle. The anarchy came to an end with the accession of Oswald, a Christian, who had been converted, not by Paulinus, but by the Celtic Church of Iona. It was this circumstance which led to the establishment of the influence of that Church in Northumbria. Oswald did not look to Rome or Canterbury for evangelists when he set to work to establish Christianity in his kingdom, but to Iona, whence, in 635 A.D., was dispatched a bishop, Aidan, who settled at Lindisfarne (Holy Island). From this time there were two influences at work among the Christians in Northumbria—that of the older and more national British Church which had survived the flood of heathen invasion ; and that of the later Catholic Church, which originated with the mission of Augustine.

The conflict between these two influences reached its height in the time of Alfred. Oswald completed the church began by Edwin : it remained under the rule of Aidan, as no evangelists were sent from the south to take the place of Paulinus, though it is said that James the Deacon continued his missionary work in the North Riding. In 642 Oswald was killed in battle, and Deira and Bernicia were again split up into two kingdoms. With this division came also religious difficulties between the Church of Iona and the Catholic Church of the south. These difficulties culminated in the Synod of Whitby, 664, at which the Catholic party, led by the great Wilfrid, perhaps the greatest of all bishops of York, defeated their opponents. After the council, Colman, then Bishop of Lindisfarne, resigned, and his successor, Tuda by name, was killed with many of his monks, by a pestilence at Lindisfarne. The ground therefore seemed to be cleared for Wilfrid. At this time Oswy was king of Bernicia, and Alchfrid his son governed Deira, probably as an independent province. Alchfrid induced Wilfrid to accept the see of York. Wilfrid at once set to work to strengthen the position of the Catholic Church and to destroy the influence of the Church of Iona in his diocese. He refused to be consecrated by a bishop of the Church of Iona, sent for that purpose to Gaul. He probably was determined not to acknowledge the supremacy of any other English see over his own. He was absent for three years, and Oswy, who favoured the Church of Iona, took advantage of his absence to appoint Ceadda (Chad) to the see of York. On his return, after being duly consecrated, Wilfrid retired without a struggle to his own monastery at Ripon. In 669, Theodore, the Archbishop of Canterbury, intervened to make peace between the two factions, and at his instigation Ceadda resigned the see in favour of Wilfrid, who at once began his great period of activity in the diocese. Whatever may be our sentimental liking for the older and more national Church of Iona, there can be no doubt that the Catholic Church was the chief support of culture, learning, and civilisation in Europe, and Wilfrid was a worthy representative of it. During his episcopate the see of York probably played the most important part it has ever taken in the history of England. At that time, more than any other, the future of learning, civilisation, and humanity was in the hands of the priests, and the English *toto divisi ab orbe* were kept in touch with the slowly reviving culture of Europe by the cosmopolitan Church of Rome. Wilfrid was undoubtedly the best representative of that culture in England. It was his object not only to Catholicise the north of England, but to educate it. He travelled continually through his vast diocese with a train of builders, artists, and teachers. His architectural activity in particular was very great. He repaired the minster at York, which had fallen almost into ruins, and built large churches at Hexham and Ripon. But he was not allowed to continue his work unopposed. Egfrith had become king of the whole of Northumbria, and a quarrel arose between him and Wilfrid.

At last the king induced Theodore, who had formerly interfered in Wilfrid's favour, but who was now perhaps jealous of his great activity and fame, to assert his supremacy over the north and to divide the great diocese of Northumbria into four bishoprics, York, Lindisfarne, Hexham, and Witherne. Theodore had received the pall; Wilfrid had not. It was therefore contended that Theodore had authority over him. Wilfrid retired to Rome to claim the support of the Pope. It was given to him, but when he returned to York, in 680, he was imprisoned and afterwards banished. Soon after Egfrith died, and Theodore, again intervening, obtained a reconciliation between Wilfrid and the new king Alchfrid. Wilfrid again became Bishop of York, but another quarrel caused him again to resign his see, and this time for good. During all this period there is no doubt that the Bishops of York were subordinate to those of Canterbury. The constant disorders to which the kingdom of Northumbria was subjected for a century, and the quarrels between bishop and king, lessened the power, both civil and ecclesiastical, of the kingdom. It was not till 734 that a bishop of York, Egbert, received the pall, which had been granted only to Paulinus, and from that time the northern archbishops seem to have been independent of Canterbury, especially after York fell into the hands of the Danes in 867. It is possible that Gregory, who directed that York and Canterbury should each appoint twelve suffragan bishops, intended to make the sees equal in every respect. The anarchy and divisions of the northern kingdom prevented this plan from being carried out. The kings of Northumbria themselves, from time to time, acknowledged the authority of Canterbury, and during the hundred years between Paulinus and Egbert that York was without a metropolitan archbishop, the Primate of Canterbury, without a rival, increased his power. With the advent of the Danes, however, Northumbria was naturally much isolated from the south, and the diocese of York, though smaller and poorer than that of Canterbury, was a rival power. In fact, until the year 1072 the archbishops of York either held themselves or appointed others to the diocese of Worcester. It was not until the Conquest that the independence of the northern bishops was seriously questioned. Under the Danish rule two of the archbishops were probably of that race—Wolfstan, appointed in 928, and Oskytel, his successor. The Danish supremacy was put an end to in 954, when Eadred incorporated Northumbria into the kingdom of England. From 867 to 1000, or after, York was ruled by an earl, either under the Danes or the kings of England. The city was important, not only as a strongly fortified place, but as a centre of commerce, and it had a large population. It had as many as 30,000 inhabitants in the tenth century. There are traces of the Danish supremacy in the language and faces of the people; in York itself Danish beads, glass, jet and amber, and carved horns have been found.

At the time of the Conquest, Aeldred was archbishop of York. After Hastings he swore allegiance to William. For this act he was bitterly reproached. It is said that he exacted a promise from William that he would treat his English and his Norman subjects alike. He crowned William at Westminster. In 1068 Edwin and Morcar, Earls of Mercia and Yorkshire, broke into rebellion. They soon submitted, but the people of York had been roused, and remained in rebellion. On the approach of the Conqueror, however, they also submitted. William built a castle in York, at the junction of the Ouse and the Foss, and garrisoned it with Normans. He then returned southwards. So soon as his back was turned, the city revolted again and besieged the castle. But William was soon upon them. He took and plundered the city, and erected another fortress on Beacon Hill. In 1069 occurred the final rebellion. A Danish fleet sailed up the Humber under Edgar, Gospatric, and Waltheof. This last calamity is said to have killed Ealdred, the archbishop. He had endeavoured to make peace between conquerors and conquered, and he saw that now a desperate struggle was inevitable. The whole of Northumbria rose as the Danes made their way up the Ouse. The Norman garrisons in York set fire to the houses near them, and the whole city was burnt down. The minster was either wholly or partially destroyed. On the site of William's fort at Beacon Hill there have lately been discovered several deposits of silver pennies of the earliest coinage of William. These were probably hidden there by the Norman garrison. After a desperate sortie, these forts were taken. Thereupon the Danes sailed away with their plunder, and the revolt suddenly came to an end. But William swore an oath of vengeance. He caught and destroyed a number of the Danes in Lincolnshire. When he reached York he found it deserted. He repaired his castles, and then

BOOTHAM BAR.

Photochrom Co. Ltd., Photo.

2

proceeded to make an example of the country round. His vengeance was so thorough that for nine years afterwards the land between York and Durham was untilled. He returned to York to keep Christmas. It is not too much to say that the north of England took centuries to recover from his vengeance. The famous library of York, which was destroyed in the fire, deserves a few words of mention. It was a fine example of the educational work of the Saxon Church. Under Egbert, and at the instigation of Bede, was founded the University of York, which soon grew to great importance. Alcuin was its chief ornament, and gave lessons there in Hebrew, Greek, and Latin. The library was formed in connection with this university, and a list of the books in it, made by Alcuin himself, has come down to us. They consist chiefly of the Fathers and of the later Latin poets, with a few books on philosophy and grammar.

Thomas of Bayeux, the first Norman archbishop, found everything at York in ruin and confusion. The minster and its outlying buildings, the library, and the university were destroyed, and only one of three canons remained in residence. He increased the number of these, and appointed a dean— there had not been one at York before—and otherwise changed the constitution of the minster. He further appointed a chancellor, or *magister scholarum*, in charge of all schools within ten miles of York. Among these was the Grammar School in the city, which still survives and flourishes, under the name of St. Peter's School. In the nave of the minster there is a window known as the Chancellor's Window, and containing a representation of Robert Riplingham, a chancellor of the fourteenth century, lecturing to his pupils. The library was never fully replaced. The books at the time of the Reformation were few, and were kept in a building close to the entrance to the south transept of the minster, and now used as the archbishop's registry. This building was erected in 1415. Most of these books are still preserved. In due course Thomas rebuilt the minster, or part of it, on a modest scale. In his episcopate the struggle for supremacy with Canterbury really began. Thomas refused to make submission to Lanfranc, Archbishop of Canterbury; but Lanfranc represented to the king that the supremacy of Canterbury was necessary as a bond of union between the south and the north. Thomas was at last compelled to submit to Lanfranc himself, though he made reserva-

B

tions with regard to his successors. In 1072 Worcester, and soon after Lindsey and Lincoln, were taken from the see of York. The abbeys of Selby and St. Oswald in Gloucester were given to the archbishop by way of some return. Meanwhile the archbishops of York also claimed supremacy over the northern bishops of the Isles and Scotland. They certainly visited and consecrated in these dioceses. After many quarrels, these pretensions were finally disposed of at Rome. In 1154 the sees of Man and Orkney were placed under the Archbishop of Drontheim, and in 1188 the whole Scottish Church was released from any subjection to York and placed under the direct control of the Pope. Only one Scottish prelate, the Bishop of Whithorn, remained a suffragan to York, but in the fourteenth century Whithorn also was lost to the archbishops, and became a part of the Scottish Church.

The Bishop of Durham remained nominally in subjection to the see of York, but in reality he was often a greater man than his superior. In 1134 the Bishopric of Carlisle was founded and placed under the authority of the archbishops. Sodor and Man afterwards fell again under his jurisdiction, and in 1542 the diocese of Chester was founded. The archbishop has now authority over nine bishoprics. But to return to Thomas. In 1071 he went with Lanfranc to Rome to receive the pall. The question of precedence was there argued, and the Pope decided in favour of Canterbury. Afterwards, at a synod held by William, it was decided that the Archbishop of York should swear allegiance to Canterbury, and must be consecrated in Canterbury Cathedral, that the diocese of York from that time should not extend south of the Humber, and that the archbishop should lose his authority over the see of Worcester. On the death of Lanfranc, however, the dispute broke out again. For four years there was a vacancy to the see of Canterbury; Anselm, the new archbishop, was consecrated by Thomas, who took the opportunity to insist that Anselm should not be styled Primate of all England. The quarrel with Canterbury remained in abeyance until Thurstan was appointed Archbishop of York (1114 A.D.). He refused to make submission to Canterbury, and the Archbishop of Canterbury was determined not to consecrate him until he submitted. There was, therefore, a deadlock. Thurstan had the support of the Pope, but he was not consecrated until 1119, when the Pope

Calixtus himself performed the ceremony at Rheims. Thurstan obtained a Bull from the Pope releasing him and his successors for ever from supremacy of Canterbury, and for a time York was triumphant.

In the reign of Henry II. the quarrel again broke out. This time the Archbishop of York, Roger Pont l'Eveque, the builder of the Norman choir of the minster, had the support of the king, who was engaged in the struggle with Becket. Roger,

Photochrom Co. Ltd., Photo.]
WALMGATE BAR.

indeed, has been bitterly reviled as an accessory to the murder of Becket. He carried on the quarrel with Richard of Canterbury, Becket's successor, and at the Council of Westminster (1176 A.D.) the rivalries of the two prelates came to a head in a ridiculous scene. The papal legate was present at the council, and the Archbishop of Canterbury seated himself at his right hand. Shortly afterwards entered the Archbishop of York, who, refusing to take a lower place, sat down in the lap of Canterbury. He was seized, beaten, and kicked for his pains.

In 1190 the people of York, incited by the priests, rose and massacred the Jews, killing nearly 500. For this they were fined by the king. The minster contributed to the ransom of Richard I., pawning a golden cross which Roger had given. The cross was afterwards redeemed.

Roger was succeeded, after an interval of ten years, by Geoffrey, the bastard son of Henry II. He quarrelled continually with John, who on one occasion fined the city of York £100 for omitting to meet him when he visited the city.

In the war between Henry III. and the barons, the archbishops Gray and Gifford took the part of the king, and owing to their efforts their diocese was little affected by the struggle.

In 1265 a quarrel broke out between the Abbey of St. Mary and the townspeople, owing to the abuse of the privilege of sanctuary possessed by the convent. Much blood was shed, and the suburb of Bootham was burnt down.

In the reign of Edward I. York played a great part in the history of England, as the king made it his capital during the war with Scotland. He was present at the installation of St. William's relics in the choir, and in 1297 he held a great Parliament there. The archbishops and clergy contributed one-fifth of their income to the expenses of the war. The Courts of the Exchequer and King's Bench were also removed from London to York, and remained there for seven years.

At this time York was a more important city than it has been at any period since the Roman occupation. It was both the civil and military capital of England, and its archbishops and prebendaries had great power. It was also, naturally, a period of great building activity. In a hundred and fifty years the whole fabric of the minster, as it now is, was erected.

Edward II. also spent much of his time at York, and in 1318 another Parliament met there. After Bannockburn the Scots made continual inroads into Yorkshire. In 1319 an army of Scots, 15,000 in number, advanced to the very gates of York. Melton, the archbishop, hastily got together 10,000 men and fell in with the Scots at Myton, on the Swale, where he was utterly routed, and narrowly escaped with his life. This battle was known in derision as the Chapter of Myton.

The quarrel between York and Canterbury was not finally settled until the time of John of Thoresby. He was one of the most remarkable of the archbishops of York. When he was made archbishop (1352) the diocese, owing to the Scottish inroads, the black death, and other causes, stood in great need of reform. Anarchy and brigandage were rife. The people were ignorant and poor, and the chief posts about the cathedral, including even the deanery, were held by Italian absentees appointed by the Pope. The ecclesiastical discipline was naturally very lax. Thoresby drew up his famous Catechism, which was translated into English verse, in 1357, and set to work to abolish the abuses caused by pluralism and immorality among the clergy. The question of precedence was settled by Innocent VI., who determined that the Archbishop of Canterbury should be styled Primate of All England, and the Archbishop of York Primate of England.

"Thus," says the sardonic Fuller, "when two children cry for the same apple, the indulgent father divides it betwixt them; yet so that he giveth the bigger and better part to the child that is his darling."

It was also settled that each archbishop should carry his cross erect in the diocese of the other, but that the Archbishop of York should send a golden image to the shrine of St. Thomas of Canterbury.

Edward III. had been married in York Minster, and there his little son, William of Hatfield, was buried. His is the only royal tomb in the minster.

In 1392 the Court of the King's Bench again sat at York. Richard II. visited the city several times. The archbishops Neville and Arundel played a great part in politics at this period. After the deposition of Richard II. a prebendary, by name Mandelyn, who bore a great resemblance to the king, personated him and headed a revolt, but he was captured and put to death. The chapter in general were strongly in favour of Richard, and three other prebendaries were imprisoned.

In 1405 occurred the rebellion, headed by Scrope, the archbishop. After he had been trapped and captured, the king had great difficulty in bringing him to trial, as the Chief Justice, Gascoyne, refused to try him. He was finally condemned in his own palace, at Bishopthorpe, and executed near to the walls of the city. Henry IV. withdrew also the liberties and privileges of the city, and the citizens had to beg for pardon on their knees with ropes round their necks. The archbishop was buried in the minster, and his tomb was much frequented by pilgrims in the north.

In 1407 the rebellion broke out again, and the citizens of York were again severely punished. In the fifteenth century the importance of York began to decline, and from that time it owes the position it still holds chiefly to its ecclesiastical eminence. Richard III. visited York several times, and gave a great cross to the minster, standing on six steps, each of which was ornamented with the figure of an angel. The figures were all of silver, and the whole was decorated with precious stones. Richard also planned the establishment of a college of 100 chaplains, and in 1485 six altars were erected for their use. But the scheme came to an end on the death of the king. York had been greatly devoted to Richard, but it submitted to Henry VII. when he made a state entry into the city in 1486, and it remained loyal in the rebellion of Lambert Simnel, when the rebels besieged the city, but were repulsed.

In the reign of Henry VIII. the importance of York was steadily declining. He only visited the city once. The whole of Yorkshire, which was no doubt poorer and more ignorant than most other counties, was much disturbed by the abolition of the monasteries and the spoiling of the churches, especially by the seizing of the head of St. William, the chief treasure of the minster. In 1536 the insurrection known as the Pilgrimage of Grace broke out, and the city willingly received the rebels. Aske, their leader, made a proclamation that all the "religions" should be reinstated in their old places; and the friars sang matins the same night. In 1557 Aske was hanged on a gallows set upon one of the bars of York. Henry entered York, and the citizens sued for pardon, which was not granted to them until 1560. Henry ordered the removal of such shrines as had not already been destroyed, and fragments of these have been found buried near the minster. Henry determined to establish his authority firmly in the north, and established the famous council which appointed the Duke of Norfolk their president. The council was held in the house of the Abbot of St. Mary's. It took away most of the powers of the Mayor and Corporation, but gave renewed importance to the city.

The diocese was much neglected during the episcopacy of Wolsey and his successor Lee. Both were statesmen rather than ecclesiastics. Indeed, it is said that Wolsey never set foot in York itself, though he was arrested at Cawood, where was one of the bishop's palaces. Lee was employed continually on missions and embassies. He happened to be in York, however, at the time of the Pilgrimage of Grace, and was seized by the rebels, carried to Pontefract, and compelled to swear support to the rebellion. The see was much impoverished in the time of Holgate, Lee's successor (1545-1554), who supported Henry in his quarrel with the Pope.

Much of the property taken by Henry was restored by Mary to Heath, the next archbishop, who was the last appointed by a papal bull with the acknowledgment of the Government. Heath was deposed by Elizabeth in 1559.

In 1569 occurred another rising in the north in favour of the old religion and of Mary Queen of Scots, under the Earls of Northumberland and Westmoreland.

In Richmondshire and the Cleveland district the new prayer-books were destroyed, and the old service restored. York itself favoured the rebels, but before it could be entered a force arrived from the south and the rebellion sank to nothing. The queen's army exacted a loan of £500 from the citizens of York. Eleven persons also in the city were sentenced to death. The Earl of Northumberland also was afterwards executed and buried in York. After the rebellion the Roman Catholics in the diocese were much persecuted. They were forced to attend the reformed services and the Holy Communion, and their priests were hunted down. Attempts also were made to abolish the Christmas mummeries and the miracle plays. The archbishop of this period, Thomas Young, is accused of plundering the estates of the church in the interests of his own family.

Charles I. had a great affection for the city and minster of York, and enriched the latter with many gifts. For instance, he gave £1000 to the chapter for the building of a new organ, and out of the same the chapter also bought some Communion plate, and a Bible and prayer-book richly bound in purple velvet and ornamented with silver-gilt plates. These latter are still preserved. He further removed certain houses and offices which had been built close to the west and south doors. He also destroyed a building which had been erected inside one of the transepts, and ordered certain seats in the choir, which hid the stalls and woodwork, to be taken away.

Charles also wrote to the Corporation in 1639, ordering them not to bring the official sword and mace into the minster, and to receive the Holy Communion there on certain fixed occasions.

The Mayor and Corporation evaded the order by entering the church with sword and mace "abased." They have never yet officially attended Holy Communion. They also had a quarrel with the dean and corporation owing to their practice of using the north aisle of the nave, known as the Lord Mayor's Walk, as a common promenade. The dean and chapter endeavoured to put a stop to this in 1632, but it continued until the end of the century.

During the Civil War York suffered less than many cathedral cities. In 1644 it was besieged by the Parliamentary troops

Photochrom Co. Ltd., Photo.]
WALMGATE BAR.

and the Scots under Fairfax and Leslie. During the siege the minster seems to have been spared as far as possible, mainly, perhaps, through the influence of Fairfax, but it did not escape entirely scatheless. Thomas Mace, the author of "Musick's Monument," was in the city during the siege, and he thus describes the way in which the minster suffered:—"The enemy was very near and fierce upon them, especially on that side the city where the church stood; and had planted their great guns mischievously against the church; with which constantly in prayer's time, they would not fail to make their hellish disturb-

Photochrom Co. Ltd., Photo.]

MICKLEGATE BAR.

ance by shooting against and battering the church; insomuch that sometimes a cannon bullet has come in at the windows and bounced about from pillar to pillar (even like some furious fiend or evil spirit) backwards and forwards and all manner of sideways, as it has happened to meet with square or round opposition amongst the pillars."

During the siege the citizens suffered much from the presence of the soldiery who were billeted upon them. Each citizen, in addition to giving free quarters to as many soldiers as possible, had to pay £2 a month for their support. The siege lasted for six weeks, and in the course of it the Marygate Tower, which was used as a record office for the whole of the north, was attacked and spoiled, all the records in it, an irreparable loss, being destroyed. The city was captured soon after Marston Moor, and the defenders obtained very good terms, marching out with all the honours of war. The citizens also were well treated. They were to enjoy all their old privileges and were to be preserved from plundering. All churches and public buildings were to be treated with respect. A Presbyterian service was at once held in the minster by the conquerors. The Corporation presented to Fairfax a butt of sack and a tun of French wine in gratitude for the good offices he had rendered them. There can be little doubt that the great amount of stained glass still remaining in the minster is owing to the control he exercised over the Parliamentarians. On October the 24th of the same year the Corporation ordered that the Solemn League and Covenant should be tendered to the aldermen and citizens. Then all the Royalist members of the Corporation were removed, and both the bishop, Williams, and the dean, Scott, were deprived of their offices. They left the country, and the dean died in a debtor's prison in 1646. Fairfax, however, who remained as governor of the city, maintained the minster in scrupulous repair, and paid all the salaries of the necessary officials. A short time before the Restoration a large sum of money was spent on the bells. It has been said, indeed, that the Puritans wished to pull down the chapter-house, but there is no authority for the statement. But the control of the minster was taken out of the hands of the chapter and given to the Corporation, and this transference was only effected by the interference of the troops. The organ given by Charles was also taken down, and silver candlesticks and other ornaments, including the brass about the shrine, perhaps, of St. William, and also the lectern in the choir, were sold for the repair of the fabric and bells. In 1646 the organ loft, the canopies over the altar in the side choir, and the font were removed. In 1647 a cushion was made of the dossal. The library was left untouched and thrown open to the public, and the keys of the minster placed in charge of the Mayor and Corporation. In place of the dean and chapter, the precentor, and chancellor—all removed—four city preachers were chosen by the Assembly of Divines, and paid out of the revenues of the minster. Meanwhile the churches in the city suffered far more than the minster itself. In 1646 all "superstitious pictures in glass" and images were ordered to be broken, and the fonts were removed. In 1648 twenty-four churches in the city were without incumbents.

After the Restoration the Corporation did everything in their power to resist a return to the old order of things, and in 1663 there was a small rebellion, as a result of which twenty-one persons were executed at York. Discontent, however, continued, and in 1682 it became necessary to appoint Sir John Reresby governor of York, with a garrison of 500 men. The governor said that York was one of the most factious towns in the kingdom. About this time, also, the dean and chapter caused a riot by issuing a proclamation forbidding the nave to be used as a promenade. They succeeded, however, in finally putting an end to the practice.

In 1686 Lady Strafford, daughter-in-law of the great Strafford, was buried in the minster. Party spirit still ran very high, and the mob rushed at the hearse and endeavoured to tear the coats of arms from it. The military was called out, and there was a sharp struggle in the minster itself.

The Catholic designs of James II. were ill received in York. His proclamation for liberty of conscience was read in hardly any of the York churches, and an attempt to stock the Corporation with Roman Catholics was resisted. At last there came a crisis. The king appointed James Smith, the Roman Catholic Bishop of Callipolis, one of his four vicars-apostolic, and in August 1688 he appeared at York. The archbishopric had been vacant for two years, and it was rumoured that the king intended to appoint Smith to the see.

York, therefore, was ripe for the revolution, and it broke out there on November 22. Lamplough of Exeter, a discreet and timely supporter of both James and William, was appointed archbishop, and Smith was attacked by the mob as he was passing through the streets in procession. His silver-gilt crozier, which had been given to him by Catharine of Braganza, was torn from him and sent to the vestry of the minster, where it still remains. It is seven feet in length. Smith fled to Wycliffe-on-Tees, where he spent the rest of his life.

Since the reign of James II., and the last serious attempt to establish the Roman Catholic religion in the country, the history of both the city and the see of York has been uneventful. The city itself has declined in importance, and is now hardly even one of the larger towns in Yorkshire. It is known and visited chiefly [for its historic interest and its minster.

Photochrom Co. Ltd., Photo.]
THE SHAMBLES.

The see has experienced only peaceful changes, and its archbishops are concerned more with questions of Church discipline than with politics. The minster has suffered two serious fires, and a restoration, carried out on the whole moderately and judiciously.

CHAPTER II

HISTORY OF THE BUILDING

THE architectural history of the minster is somewhat vague and uncertain, and has been the subject of several disputes. It will be as well, perhaps, before entering into details, to give a table of approximate dates, both of the different parts of the minster as it now stands and of the buildings which preceded it. These dates are mostly sanctioned by the authority of Professor Willis.

Edwin's Wooden Chapel	627 A.D.
Edwin's Minster begun	(circ.) 628
,, ,, finished by Oswald	(circ.) 635
,, ,, repaired by Wilfrid	(circ.) 699
,, ,, burnt down (?)	741
Albert rebuilds Minster (?)	767-780
Minster wholly or partially burnt	1069
Nave, Transepts, and perhaps Choir, built by Thomas	(circ.) 1080
Choir and Crypt rebuilt by Roger	1154-1181
Present South Transept built	1230-1241 (circ.)
,, North Transept ,,	1241-1260
,, Nave built	1291-1324
,, Chapter-House built	1320 (?)
,, West Front of Nave built	1338
Vault of Nave built	(circ.) 1354
Presbytery (or eastern part of Choir) built	1361-1370 (circ.)
Choir (west of High Altar) built	1380-1400 (circ.)
Central Tower built	1400-1423 (circ.)
South-West Bell Tower built	1433-1447
North-West Bell Tower built	1470-1474
Choir injured by fire	1829
Choir repaired	(circ.) 1832
Nave injured by fire	1840
Nave repaired	1841
South Transept restored	1875

It will be seen that it is doubtful whether the fire of 741 and the rebuilding of 767-780 mentioned by historians refer to the minster at all.

HISTORY OF THE BUILDING

The fact that a wooden chapel was erected for the baptism of Edwin in 627 seems to show that no Christian church had remained at York from Roman days, as at Canterbury; this chapel, therefore, is the first Christian building in York of which we have any definite record. The church of stone with which it was immediately replaced was finished by Oswald, after the death of Edwin in battle; whose head was carried thither and placed in the Chapel of St. Gregory. It has been supposed that there are remains of this original stone church in the crypt.

In sixty years Edwin's church had fallen into great disrepair. It was restored by Archbishop Wilfrid about 669. The following account of the dilapidated condition of the building as he found it is taken from a versified life of Wilfrid, ascribed to Frithegode, a monk of the tenth century:—

> Ecclesiae vero fundamina cassa vetustae,
> Culmina dissuto violabant trabe palambes,
> Humida contrito stillabant assere tecta;
> Livida nudato suggrundia pariete passa
> Imbricibus nullis, pluriae quacunque vagantur,
> Pendula discissis fluitant laquearia tignis,
> Fornice marcebant cataractae dilapidato.

Wilfrid glazed the windows, repaired the holes, painted and decorated, and, strange to say, whitewashed the building.

We now come to the first disputed point in the history of the minster. In the chronicle of Richard Hovenden it is stated that *Monasterium in Eboraca Civitate Succensum est nono Kalendas Maii Feria prima*—that is to say, that a church was burnt down in the city of York on Sunday the 23rd of April 741 A.D. It has been contended that the word *monasterium* need not of necessity mean the minster, that the word *civitas* may perhaps mean the diocese, the ecclesiastical state, and not the city of York, and that, therefore, the church mentioned may be not the minster, but some other large church in the city or diocese of York. Professor Willis is of opinion that this is probably the case.

In the poem of Alcuin or Flaccus Albinus, there is a passage speaking of a church built by Albert (767-780), in the following terms:—

> Ast nova Basilicae mirae structura diebus
> Praesulis hujus erat jam caepta, peracta, sacrata,

> Haec nimis alta domus solidis suffulta columnis
> Suppositae quae stant curvatis arcubus, intus
> Emicat egregiis laquearibus atque fenestris
> Pulchraque porticibus fulget circumdata multis,
> Plurima diversis retinens solaria tectis,
> Quae triginta tenet variis ornatibus aras.

It is plain that this church, wherever it was, and the poem does not mention its locality, was a very important one. It was very lofty, and had many porches, or apses (*porticus* may mean either), and thirty altars.

Just before this passage in the poem there is an account of altars set up by the archbishop, probably in the cathedral. Professor Willis thinks that if the church referred to immediately after were the cathedral, an account of altars set up in it would not be given before an account of the building of the church itself. But, as Professor Freeman points out, it is most improbable that two writers, the chronicler and Flaccus Albinus, should allude to a church other than the minster without giving its name. It is, of course, just possible that Albert set up his altars before rebuilding the cathedral, in which case Professor Willis' contention would lose its force. It is curious that no other chronicler mentions either the fire or the rebuilding of the church, but this omission would be almost equally strange whether the building in question were the minster or some important church in the diocese.

On the whole, therefore, it is perhaps most probable that the church referred to by Flaccus Albinus was the minster. If that is so, this church remained until it was ruined by the Danes in 1069. Then it was certainly either wholly or partially burnt down. Thomas, the first Norman archbishop, appointed in 1070, found the minster, the city, and the diocese, all waste and desolate. At first he was satisfied with roofing in what remained of the cathedral and otherwise restoring it as best he could. Afterwards, before 1080, he began to rebuild it. It is uncertain whether he rebuilt the whole church, or merely the nave and transepts.

Stubbs on this point seems to give two different accounts. "Thomas," he states, "restored the canons of the church after he had rebuilt it as well as he could. Afterwards he says, " He built the church as it now is from its foundations."

Probably, this first passage refers to the immediate repairs which Thomas found necessary in 1070, and the second to his ultimate rebuilding of the church.

William of Malmesbury says that he began the church from its foundations and finished it. In the face of this positive testimony it is probable that Thomas built not only the nave but the choir. That he did so has been doubted, because the choir of his day was undoubtedly a very small one, and was afterwards demolished by Roger. It must, however, be remembered that Lanfranc rebuilt Anselm's Norman choir at Canterbury in the same way. It is very likely that Thomas was forced by necessity to plan his work on as modest a scale as possible, and that the pride of Roger would not allow the choir of his minster to remain one of the smallest in the cathedrals of England.

The minster, as Thomas left it, was utterly unlike the present church. The nave was probably shorter than the present one, and was certainly twenty feet narrower. This was discovered after the fire of 1840, when remains of the side aisle walls of Thomas's nave were discovered. There are no data for the number of piers in this nave or for the position of the west front.

The tower certainly stood on the site of the present tower, as Roman ashlaring has been discovered on the north-west side of the north-west tower pier, above the vault of the side aisle, and also portions of a shaft with a base, which probably belonged to the Norman clerestory. It will be seen that the present piers supporting the central tower contain cores of Norman work recased in Perpendicular times.

The transepts of Thomas's church appear to have been without aisles. The remains in the crypt show that there were two eastern apses to these transepts close to the central tower, and Professor Willis deduces from the position of these apses that they left no room for eastern aisles. There is no instance in existence of a transept having western without eastern aisles. One may therefore conclude that aisles were entirely wanting. Professor Willis thinks it possible that an additional pair of apses may have existed on the east side of these transepts, to the north and south respectively of these already discovered. This was certainly the case in St. Mary's Abbey.

As has been mentioned, considerable doubts still exist as to the size and character of the choir of Thomas's church.

C

On the one hand we have positive testimony that Thomas rebuilt the whole church; on the other, the walls of the crypt, as they existed up to the time of Roger's choir, are a part of the Saxon church. Their masonry is Saxon, and they mark the lines of a chancel far too narrow to have been that of Thomas, even if we suppose that his choir was necessarily small, from the want of funds at his command, and the wasted condition of the diocese.

This would seem to support the theory that Thomas left the Saxon choir as it was, and contented himself with rebuilding the ruined nave and transepts. In that case, of course, the Saxon choir remained until the time of Roger.

The alternate theory is that Thomas rebuilt an enlarged, but still a small, choir, leaving the Saxon crypt as it remains to this day; and that even this choir proved too small for the magnificent ideas of Roger, who utterly demolished it to make room for his own great building, leaving no trace of it above ground. This is the more probable supposition, and it is supported by the fact that the inner wall of the crypt is composed of fragments of masonry, buildings, etc., of early Norman date, which might well be parts of Thomas's choir, if it was destroyed, as we suppose. Some of the stones are covered with white plaster, showing they are parts of the interior of a building, and they are of the same red sandstone as the remains of the transept apse, which was undoubtedly built by Thomas.

As has been said, the choir of the minster remained unusually small for so important a church. The eleventh and twelfth centuries were periods of great activity in church building, and many of the Norman architects planned their works on a vast scale. With the examples of Durham, Winchester, and St. Albans before them, it was natural that the archbishops of the Metropolitan Church of York should be dissatisfied with the size of their own choir. It fell to the lot of Roger, the rival of Thomas à Becket, to rebuild it. The date of his nave is approximately 1154-1181. The remains of his work in the crypt show that it was in the latest style of Norman architecture and considerably influenced by Flambard's work at Durham, with channeled and fluted pillars. The detail appears to have been richer and later in character even than Flambard's. The outer wall of the crypt shows the dimensions of this choir. It was square at the end, and had flanking towers—two bays

YORK MINSTER.

From an old Print.

from the east—which served as transepts inside. The eastern transepts of the present choir still keep the position and tradition of these towers. The aisle probably ran round the east end as at Romsey and Byland. The two bays east of the tower were wider than the others. Roger, it should be said, had been Archdeacon of Canterbury, and he was therefore well acquainted with the " glorious Choir of Conrad " built by Anselm. There is much in the planning of his work to show that he was influenced by the example of Conrad's choir.

At the end of the twelfth century the minster was utterly unlike the present building. Except in the crypt, and in certain parts of the nave and tower not visible to the casual observer, there are no vestiges of the work of the earlier builders. There is now no Norman work to be seen in the minster itself, and in 1200, nave, choir, transepts, and towers were all Norman. Of these the transepts appear to have been the poorest part. They were probably short, and had no aisles. The nave also was of rude Early Norman character. The Early English architects having determined, probably, to rebuild the nave and transepts, made a beginning with the transepts about 1230. Roger's choir, only finished about fifty years before, no doubt seemed to them grand enough. The transepts were built on a totally different scale to the rest of the church as it then stood. They were both longer and broader, and they had aisles on each side of them. No doubt the object of this was to get a standard for the ultimate rebuilding of the nave. The greater width of these transepts made it difficult to join their aisles with those of the nave and choir, and were the cause of a curious and daring expedient, which will be described in the architectural account of the building. The south transept was the first to be rebuilt. It is the work of Walter de Gray, archbishop from 1216 to 1265, who was buried under an arch of his own building, in a tomb which still remains the most beautiful, perhaps, in the minster.

The north transept seems to have been begun as soon as the south was finished; it is said to have been the work of John Romeyn, or the Roman, an Italian, and the treasurer of York. Walter de Gray probably also had a large part in the building of them. These transepts are the earliest part of the existing minster. John Romeyn also built an Early English central tower in place of Thomas's Early Norman tower. It remained for John Romeyn the younger, son of the treasurer, and archbishop from 1286 to 1296, to begin the rebuilding of the nave. It was planned on a far larger scale than the old nave, and was wider even than the Early English transepts. The old nave had been 83 feet wide, the transepts were 95, and the new nave 103. The difference in width between the transepts and the new nave is in the aisles. The plan of the transepts had no influence on the plan of the nave. The large triforium, small clerestory, and moderate-sized main arches give way to a large clerestory, large main arches, and practically non-existent triforium. These are unusual proportions in English Churches of that period. At Ely, Westminster, Beverley, and many other places, the proportions of Norman or Early English work influenced those of the later Decorated and Perpendicular.

The records of the building of the nave are somewhat scanty. Stubbs tells us that the foundation stone was laid on April 6, 1291, and that it was begun on the south side towards the east. It has been supposed that the chief object of making the new nave so much wider and loftier than its predecessor, was that it might be built round the old work without interfering with its utility.

But a petition, dated 1298, states that the old nave had long since fallen (*diu est corruita*). If this were so there was no object in refraining from disturbing the old work. It is uncertain whether the nave had been purposely destroyed, or had fallen of its own weight. It may be, though we have no record of the fact, that Thomas's Norman tower fell down, as did so many Norman central towers, destroying with it some part of the nave, and so made the rebuilding of that part of the church necessary.

The nave is fully developed geometrical Decorated work. It is loftier than the transepts, and its roof is low pitched. The main part of the rebuilding seems to have been done between 1298 and 1320. The indenture for glazing the great west window is still extant, and is dated 1338. The nave must have been roofed before this.

The vault was probably intended to be stone, but the great width of the building seems to have made the builders afraid, and they erected a vault of wood, but shaped and ribbed to look like stone. The outer walls of the clerestory, and the pinnacles of the south side of the nave show vestiges of flying buttresses. It is uncertain whether these were merely intended when a stone vault was projected, or whether they were actually erected, and afterwards, being unnecessary for the support of a wooden vault, were allowed to fall into disrepair. There are no flying buttresses on the north side, and the pinnacles are much smaller.

The west front was undoubtedly the latest part of the work to be finished, except the vault. The lowest stages, though geometrical in style, are later in character than the nave itself. The great west window, and the upper stages are of florid curvilinear Gothic. The west front is said to have been finished, and the great west window glazed by Archbishop Melton, who gave 500 or 600 marks to the fabric in 1338. The church was vaulted in 1354; Archbishop Thoresby is said to have given the wood. Before the beginning of the nave, the relics of St. William had been carried into the choir, and installed there with great pomp. The offerings of the faithful at his shrine helped to defray the expense of the building. Further funds were gained by means of indulgences granted by successive archbishops. The houses of Vavasour and Percy gave wood and stone, and statues of their representatives were placed over the main porch of the west front.

The date of the chapter-house, and the passage connecting it with the north transept is disputed. Browne thinks it was begun about 1280, and finished about 1340. He partly bases his contention on the fact that the Acts of the Chapter from 1223 to 1300 are given *in Capitulo Eborum.* After 1300 *in Capitulo Ecclesiae,* or *in loco Capitulari ipsius Ecclesiae.* After 1342 *in domo Capitulari.* From this he argues that up to 1342 the chapter-house was not in existence, or unfinished, but that it was in use from that date. The geometrical character of the tracery, and the Purbeck marble shafts used in the chapter-house might seem to support that view. Professor Willis, however, considers there is little significance in the difference in the phrases used. *In capitulo* simply means "in chapter," and *in loco capitulari* and *in domo capitulari* are vague phrases which may either mean a chapter-house, or a place used for the sittings of the chapter. At any rate, he thinks the chapter-house was not begun until after 1320, and the passage leading to it is still later. If this

THE WEST FRONT IN 1810

is the case, however, there is no reason why the chapter-house should not have been finished in 1342, and that would account for the change of phrase in the Acts. Though, at first sight, the building appears to be Early Decorated in style, on a closer examination it will be seen that the slender mouldings, the character of the carvings, and the details, especially on the outside, all point to a later date. It is curious, however, that if the building was not begun until after 1320, the tracery was not curvilinear, as in the great west windows, and the middle windows of the towers built about the same time. Perhaps, however, the geometrical forms were found to give the greater support, necessary owing to the absence of a central pillar. On the whole, the evidence of details, particularly of the foliage in the beautiful arcading inside the chapter-house, seem to point to its not having been begun until 1320 or later.

In 1362 John of Thoresby became archbishop. The times were unpropitious for building. Yorkshire was suffering much from the black death, there was great poverty among the peasantry, and the diocese was in great need of discipline and reform. Thoresby gave himself up for nine years to this work, and in 1361 he thought the time had come for the rebuilding of the choir. We have already seen how at York, one great work led to another. The transepts were rebuilt that they might be in harmony with the grandeur of Roger's choir, the nave that it might not be eclipsed by the transepts; and now it was contended that the choir must not be inferior to the rest of the church. Therefore, on the 20th of July 1361, it was resolved by the archbishop and chapter that "It was right that every church whatsoever should agree in the fitting decoration of each particular part, and that the choir in particular, where the holy sacrifice of the mass took place, should be especially rich in ornament." Thereupon they decided to rebuild the choir. The foundation stone was laid on the 30th July 1361, and the work was begun at the extreme east end. There was a very good reason for this procedure. The design of the new choir, both as to size and the planning of the bays, was modelled on that of the nave. It was Thoresby's object to build the largest and most magnificent choir in England. It was therefore both wider, loftier, and longer than that of Roger's, and beginning at the east end it was possible to complete almost the whole of the portion east of the altar as it now stands—that is to say, the presbytery, without interfering with Roger's choir. While, therefore, the presbytery was being built, the service of the church was still carried on in Roger's choir, and only the aisles behind Roger's east end were destroyed. Even when the four bays of the presbytery were completed, say about 1370, it was possible to continue the aisles of the new choir proper without interfering with Roger's work, except to pull down the towers flanking it, so much wider was the new building than the old. Even Roger's transepts did not extend beyond the aisle walls of the new choir, and their place was taken by the present eastern transepts, which are each merely a bay of the aisle, raised to the same height as the vault of the choir itself, and open to the choir from top to bottom.

There has been a dispute whether or no this presbytery was completed in Thoresby's lifetime. According to Stubbs, Thoresby provided tombs for six of his predecessors, and placed them in the choir in front of the lady chapel—that is to say, in the presbytery.

He also says that *Idem Archiepiscopus . . . Capellam . . . Virginis Mariae Mirabili arte Sculpturae atque notabili pictura peregit.*

The building must certainly have been roofed before it was decorated, and if Stubbs is accurate, and there is no reason to suppose that he is not, the work was completed by Thoresby. Thoresby died in 1373, and if he finished the presbytery, there was a gap of seven or eight years between its completion and the beginning of the choir. There is internal evidence to support this presumption. The presbytery, though Perpendicular in its main features, shows many traces of the transition from the curvilinear Decorated to the Perpendicular style, especially in the tracery of the great east window and the clerestory windows. In the choir proper these traces have vanished, and the work, though apparently of the same character as that in the presbytery, is altogether Perpendicular. A lapse of ten years in the continuity of the work would account for this change, and becomes still more probable when we consider that the circumstances of the time were not favourable for great expenditure on building. The presbytery had been completed unusually quickly. Indeed, we know that £627 were spent upon it in one year, and this was an unusual amount. The average expenditure, for instance, on the choir of Ely was £318. It was natural, therefore, that there should be a halt to collect further funds. The work of the choir itself proceeded much more slowly. There was a complaint in 1390 on the archbishop's visitation—*quod fabrica ecclesiae negligenter tardatur*—and it was not roofed in until 1400.

The contract for the glazing of the great east window is December 10, 1405—that is to say, thirty years and more from the date of its construction. But there is nothing unusual in this. It was customary before filling windows with stained glass to cover them with linen cloth which admitted a sufficient amount of light, or to glaze them with plain glass; and it was only natural that a long time should elapse before stained glass could be supplied to the largest window in the world. Burying was begun at the east end soon after 1400, and Scrope was buried there in 1405. Bowet's monument also was erected there in 1415, while he was still alive.

A new high altar was projected in 1418, and the new crypt was fitted with iron work and paved in the same year. The building of the choir had caused a subsidence in the crypt, so the work of Roger and others was broken into fragments and patched together, older capitals being placed on Roger's pillars, in the condition in which we now see it. Nothing is known of the history of the vaults of the choir and eastern transepts. Like those of the nave and transepts, they are of wood, though of the same shape and design as a stone vault.

The great central tower was erected between 1400 and 1423. Hitherto there had been the Early English tower of the elder John Romeyn, supported by Norman piers which, perhaps, had received a partial casing of Early English stonework. These piers were afterwards recased, not simultaneously, but as the arches between them were erected, in the following manner:—

Taking the south-western pier for an example: when the present nave was begun, the western face of the pier was cased with masonry, so that three parts still remained Norman; when the Decorated arch[1] in the transept was erected south of it, it

---

[1] For the explanation of the erection of this Decorated arch, see the architectural account of the transepts.

received a further Decorated casing on its south side ; when

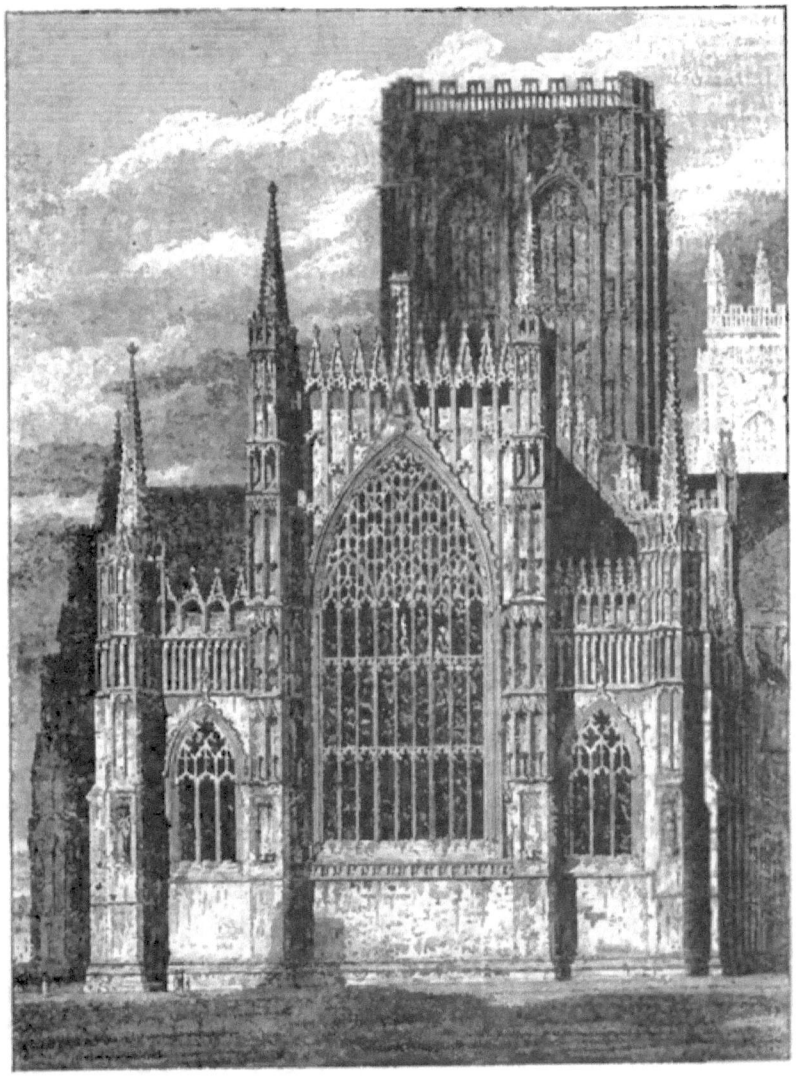

THE EAST END. From Britton.

the central tower was built, its northern and eastern faces were cased with Perpendicular masonry : so, in the case of the north and south-eastern piers, their eastern faces were completely cased when the choir was built, their western only when the tower was in course of erection. To this day it may be seen that there is no bond between the different periods of masonry, and that the courses are at different levels.

The piers were probably completely recased by 1409.

Nothing is known of the elder Romeyn's tower, or the manner in which the present one replaced it. A great part of the new work has been attributed to Walter Skirlawe, Bishop of Durham. It will be seen it is of the same character as the lower part of the central tower at Durham. It has never been finished, as the corners and the condition of the masonry at the top still show, but it is impossible to say whether it was intended to receive another storey, and if so, of what character that other storey was to be. At one time, as may be seen in old engravings, it had a turret in one corner, 24 feet high; this was probably destroyed in the last century.

The south-west bell tower was built probably betweeen 1433 and 1447, the north-west between 1470 and 1474. They are thus both Perpendicular in style.

At the end of the fifteenth century, therefore, the minster as we now see it was fully built. Since that date it has suffered no changes of importance, and the record is only one of occasional damage from fires or fanaticism, and of necessary restorations.

The minster suffered to a certain extent at the restoration, and in a less degree at the hands of the Puritans. In 1734 the nave was repaved. Several tombs were found when the old pavement was removed, and relics taken from them and deposited with the other treasures of the minster.

On the 2nd February 1829, Jonathan Martin, a brother of the apocalyptic painter, John Martin, and a religious maniac, hid himself during evening service behind the tomb of Archbishop Greenfield in the north transept, and when the church was shut up for the night set fire to the choir. The flames were not extinguished until the stalls, the organ, and the vault had been entirely destroyed. The actual stonework and carving of the choir were considerably injured, and the glass of the great east window itself only just avoided destruction. Martin escaped through a window of the transept, but was quickly captured, and discovered to be insane. The restoration, carried on by Smirke, was begun in 1832, and on the whole was fairly done. At any rate, the authorities of the minster may console themselves with the knowledge that it was absolutely necessary. The stalls were a reproduction, as exact as possible, of the old woodwork, but the design of the throne and pulpit are original, and not successful. The cost of the restoration was £65,000, most of which was contributed by subscription. Timber, to the value of £5000, was given by the State, and Sir Edward Vavasour, following the example of his ancestor of the fourteenth century, supplied the stone.

Another fire broke out on the 30th May 1840. It began in the south-west tower, and is said to have been caused by some workmen who were repairing the clock. The whole tower, excepting its shell, including the bells, was destroyed, and the fire was not extinguished until the wooden vault of the nave had been burnt. The restoration on this occasion cost £23,000, and was finished in a year, under the superintendence of Sydney Smirke, son of the former restorer.

In 1871 the south transept was discovered to be in a dilapidated, and, indeed, a dangerous condition, and the advice of Street was asked on the question of restoring it. In his report he stated that the design of the clerestory, constructed as it was of two thin walls, was not strong enough for the weight it had to support, even though the vault was of wood. The whole wall of the transept had given way, and the clerestory, in particular, was in a very bad condition. It became necessary, therefore, to rebuild the side walls of the clerestory and the flying buttresses under the steep roofs of the aisles, to remove the heavy slates from the roof, and to renew the pinnacles.

On investigation, it was discovered that the inside portion of the walls had been made up of stone chippings without cement. It is curious that builders in the thirteenth century, whose system of ornament was most profuse and thorough, often scamped the more important details of structure. At Peterborough, no less than at York, instances have been discovered of what would, in these days, be called jerry-building.

The walls were rebuilt with solid masonry, held together by Portland cement, and strengthened by wrought-iron bars; the Purbeck marble shafts were in places renewed; the groining of the vault was stripped of the whitewash which concealed its material; the lath and plaster work of the vault between the groins was removed, and replaced by oak boarding; the bosses were gilded, and picked out with vermilion paint.

The cost in all of this restoration was about £20,000. In the course of it it was discovered that there were many remains of tombs and coffins under the pavement, but they have not yet been thoroughly explored.

The reredos, made of terra-cotta and wood, was designed by Street, the figures by Tinworth.

Modern stained glass windows have from time to time been placed in the minster. In the last century a certain Pickett patched and rearranged much of the older glass.

CHAPTER III

THE EXTERIOR

YORK MINSTER consists of a nave of eight bays and a choir of nine. It has a large central tower and two western towers. The main transepts project three bays from the nave and choir. There are also two eastern transepts four bays west of the east end, which do not project beyond the aisles of the choir. The chapter-house lies to the east of the northern transept, and is connected with it by a lofty passage projecting three bays from the transept. The east end of the cathedral is square, as in most English Gothic churches. The best views are to be obtained from the north, especially from the walls, which will be most conveniently ascended at Bootham Bar, or from the extreme northern corner of the close. From the walls the whole of the vast bulk of the minster may be seen, broken by the great central tower and the lofty cap of the chapter-house. Other English cathedrals are more finely placed, several are richer in ornament, one or two have a more delicately varied outline. None are so stately and so magnificent; and there is hardly a church in Europe that appears so vast as the minster viewed from the north. Compared with it the great French cathedrals, with their stilted roofs so often unbroken, except by a small flèche and with their outlines concealed in a crowd of flying buttresses, are apt to look short and huddled when seen from a distance.

The low-pitched roof of the minster, the absence of flying buttresses, and the simple and tranquil front of the north transept, give the building an air of masculine and stately repose, and of perfect finish seldom to be found in foreign churches; while the apparent uniformity of style, though the architecture is of three different periods, frees it from the picturesque inconsequence of many English cathedrals. Yet neither inside nor outside does the minster appear to be the expression of the spiritual aspirations of a people. It represents rather the secular magnificence, the temporal power of a Church, that has played a great part in the history of the nation. The archbishops of York have been forced by circumstances to be militant prelates, contending with Canterbury for precedence, leading armies against the Scotch, sometimes even heading rebellions against the king; and in their cathedral they have expressed their ambition and their pride.

The West Front.—The west front of York Minster is free from the two faults most common to the façades of most English cathedrals. It is not a mere undistinguished ending to the church, like those at Norwich and Winchester, and it is not a magnificent misrepresentation of the height or width of the building itself, like the west fronts at Peterborough and Lincoln. Most of the English cathedrals are not lofty or wide enough to give opportunities for an impressive façade, unless they are fronted with a mere screen of masonry; but this is not the case at York. No other Gothic church in England is so wide, and only Westminster Abbey is as lofty. The builder, therefore, was not tempted to any expedient to conceal the dimensions of his church, and so the front consists of the natural end of the nave, of which a great part is filled by the west window, with a gable above it representing the space between the vault and the roof, and with the porch below it. It is flanked by two towers built in front of the aisles, with two smaller porches at the base of each. The three divisions of the west front are marked by buttresses, prominent and richly ornamented, one on each side of the west window and two at the external corners of the towers. The buttresses, covered with niches and panelling, grow narrower and less prominent as they rise, until they are cut short with three cornered caps some feet below the battlements of the towers. The central window and the principal entrance are surrounded with niches, and there is an elaborate gable above each of them. The west front exhibits three different styles; the lowest part, containing the porches and the west windows of the aisle, being of the geometrical Decorated style; the middle portion, including the great west window, the gables above it, and the middle windows of the towers of the later or curvilinear Decorated; and the towers above the roof, Perpendicular of the fifteenth century. The central gable and the great west window are almost flamboyant

THE EXTERIOR

in their decoration. A battlement immediately above the central window runs right across the front. The niches on the buttresses are in four storeys, and those on the central part of the front in six, of varying heights. There is also a row of niches on the towers immediately above the ornamental gable of the aisle windows, and the upper part of each tower is covered with niches. The greater part of these niches above the two lowest rows do not appear to have ever contained sculpture. The bases of the lowest row of niches are richly ornamented with foliage. The main entrance, though small, is extraordinarily beautiful. It consists of a single arch, divided into two smaller cusped arches by a central pillar with a circular opening above it, glazed and filled with six divisions of cusped tracery. Above the main arch is a gable, in which are five niches, the central one containing the figure of an archbishop. It is uncertain whether this is Archbishop John Romeyn, who began the nave, or Archbishop Melton, who finished the west front and glazed the central window. On either side of the gable

Photochrom Co. Ltd., Photo.]
THE WEST FRONT—MAIN ENTRANCE.

are statues of the Percy and Vavasour, who gave the wood and stone necessary for the building of the nave. These statues, and the greater part of the porch, have been restored. But even after restoration the fine proportions and delicate workmanship of the porch are evident. The slender shafts supporting the arches are well grouped and contrasted. The capitals, though characteristically small, are most delicate, and the mouldings are admirably varied with foliage, figures, canopies, and brackets for statues, formal decoration, and courses of plain stone. These mouldings contain the history of Adam and Eve. Even the porches at Sienna and Orvieto, though made of far more costly materials, can hardly be more beautiful than was this porch at the time of its completion. There is but little other statuary remaining on the west front. A few figures of saints remain in the upper niches of the buttresses, and there are fragments of sculpture on some of the lowest. The towers are 201 feet high, and are uniform in design. The front of each contains three large windows; the highest, Perpendicular in style, containing three lights; the middle, curvilinear Decorated, containing four; and the lowest, the west windows of the aisle, being geometrical Decorated, and containing three lights. The middle windows to the north and south are of very curious half geometrical, half curvilinear tracery. The highest and lowest windows of the towers have ornamented gables above them, the lowest being triangular, the upper ogee-shaped. The towers are topped with large battlements and pinnacles.

It will be seen, therefore, that this west front is planned on the most regular lines and the most ambitious scale. True, some French façades are loftier, as at Amiens for instance, but, as Professor Freeman has pointed out, the effect aimed at at York is one of breadth rather than of height, and it is an advantage that the front is not too high for the towers to rise some way above it. It is also richly decorated and well proportioned in the mass, and yet nearly every one, on first seeing it, must be struck by its curious ineffectiveness when its height and breadth, its regular outline, and profusion of ornament are considered. To tell the truth, the English architects have here endeavoured to rival the French on their own ground, and have not succeeded. The English cathedral, as has been said, was not usually planned on such lines as to make a sumptuous façade possible. Throughout the whole course of English Gothic architecture, the treatment of the west end is curiously hesitating and arbitrary. Sometimes it is altogether unambitious, as at Winchester and Norwich; sometimes boldly illogical, as at Lincoln or Peterborough; and at Salisbury, where everything else is beautiful, it is altogether unsatisfactory. In all these cases circumstances were against the architect, but at York there was every opportunity for a great architectural triumph. Yet the designer was not able to throw off his English timidity, to forget the small English features to which he was used, and to conceive his front as a gigantic whole.

To begin with, he made his west window so large that every other important feature of the central division of the front had to be sacrificed to make room for it. In the great French façades the customary circular window leaves ample space for vast porches below it. These are pushed forward to a level with the great flanking buttresses, so that the actual wall of the church above it appears to be recessed. As the side porches fronting the aisles are on the same level with the main porch, the bottom part of the front is bound together, and the divisions of nave and aisle, emphasised above by the prominent buttresses, are minimised below. This arrangement gives at once unity and variety to the whole design. The towers do not appear to be external additions rising from the ground, but an integral part, the very crown and flower, in fact, of the whole design.

At York the central window is so large that it leaves but little room below it for the porch. This porch, though exquisite in itself, is not pushed forward, but flat with the wall, and appears a mere hole cut in the surface. It has necessarily no connection with the entrances to the aisles; and the finest feature of the great French façades is wanting. But the size of the west window has other disastrous effects. It would have been difficult, almost impossible, to assimilate an opening so large, and of such an elaborate pattern, to the rest of the design, and hardly an effort even has been made to do so. It appears, therefore, like the porches, to have been cut bodily out of the front without regard for the rest of the plan, and its acute arch harmonises badly with the gable above it. No doubt the designer saw the fault; he placed an acute ornamental gable above the window, rising to the top of the front, and he covered the actual gable of the roof with flamboyant tracery of the same character as that on the window; but, by so doing, he merely weakened the contrast between tracery and bare spaces of masonry so necessary to every great design.

The weakness of the central division is not made up for by any excellence in the towers. These, though fine on their lower storeys, are strangely feeble above. They are, in fact, the worst part of the minster, and have been condemned by all critics, from Mr Ruskin downwards. In most towers of this kind there are two windows above and a single one below. At York the three storeys of single windows give the design an air of monotony and weakness. Further, the highest window is not only far too large, but is placed too low. Like the great west window, it appears to have been cut out of the wall. It is also peculiarly unfortunate that the buttresses should die into the wall below the pinnacles. Where a tower is buttressed, it is a natural and logical device to make the pinnacles a continuation of the buttresses. Here both pinnacles and buttresses, unusually prominent and elaborate, do not seem to be an integral part of the design. They have been called a kind of architectural confectionery, and the criticism is just. The fact that the battlements and pinnacles project a few inches over the walls of the towers, only adds to the air of weakness and instability of the whole. Nowhere else surely has a Gothic architect approached so closely to the ideals of his "churchwarden" imitators of the beginning of this century.

But these faults, though serious enough, do not include everything that can be said against the west front of the minster. Gothic churches have often been noble and triumphant works of art in spite of errors almost as grave. Unfortunately the west front suffers from a tendency first beginning to show itself in the middle of the fourteenth century, which afterwards became the most serious drawback of the whole Perpendicular style. It is not only because the porches do not project that it appears flat and thin. The west front of Notre Dame at Paris has no projecting porches, yet the alternations of bare spaces of wall and of rich and deep masses of carving, the strong horizontal lines, and the deep-set windows, give it a boldness and strength altogether wanting at York. Like all Norman and earlier Gothic work, it has this great merit, often most strongly felt by people who are quite unable to explain it, that the design seems to emphasise, and to be dictated by, the

materials in which it is carried out. The Norman architect never forgot for a moment—he was not skilful enough to forget—that he was building with stone. So he did not conceive of his west front as a flat space to be ornamented, but as a wall to be built, and naturally his ornament followed and emphasised the main lines of his building. His single pillars, with their heavy capitals, bore witness that they were made of great stones piled one on the top of the other; his simple windows were merely openings in the wall to let in light.

But as masons grew more skilful, and designers more sophisticated, they found it pleasant to play with their material; to turn their single pillars into bundles of clustered shafts; to fill their windows with tracery, structural at first, but afterwards as free and fantastic as lacework. The result is often beautiful. The method gave the freest play to the artist's invention, but it had its dangers, and they are exemplified at York. There the designer has evidently regarded his west front as a large space of wall to be played with, to be decorated much as if it were a piece of embroidery, and, in his anxiety to decorate it richly, he has lost his sense of unity and proportion. He has forgotten to use his ornament merely to emphasise the main lines of the structure. Where this is done, where the ornament is massed on the porches, on the windows, and on the lines dividing the storeys, the rest of the façade may be left alone. The bare spaces of masonry only serve to give relief to the decoration. But at York the main lines are so neglected, they offer so little opportunity for decoration, that the designer was afraid to leave his walls plain, lest the whole should appear lean and cold. He has, therefore, spun his tracery and panelling over the whole surface. Nowhere can the eye rest on a plain piece of wall; everywhere it is fidgeted by monotonous rows of niches and mouldings. In fact, it may be compared to an etching so full of unnecessary details that composition, balance of mass, and beauty of line are all smothered in them. And yet there is much to be said on the other side. The mere size—the height and width—go far to make the front impressive; and the detail, even now when so much of it has been restored, is usually beautiful. If it is not great architecture, it is at least living architecture, and as such infinitely superior to the most scholarly works of the Gothic revival. It is only when we compare it to the magnificent west fronts of France that we are inclined to regret that it has not rivalled them.

The north side of the exterior of the nave differs from the south in several particulars. Thus, on the south the aisle buttresses are crowned by lofty pinnacles having at their bases niches, in some of which statues still remain. These pinnacles appear to have been originally connected with the wall of the nave by flying buttresses, traces of which still exist, both on the walls and the pinnacles. In Hollar's engraving, in a later print in Dugdale's "Monasticon" (1817), and in Willis's "Cathedrals" (1742), these buttresses are represented as existing, but the accuracy of the pictures in these books cannot be trusted. It is possible that a beginning only was made of these flying buttresses, and that when it was decided to place a wooden vault on the cathedral, they were discontinued as being unnecessary. At any rate, there are no pinnacles to the aisle buttresses on the north side, and, consequently, no flying buttresses. The plainer style of the north side was perhaps owing to the fact that a great part of it was concealed by the archbishop's palace, yet at the present day it is certainly more beautiful than the south. It closely resembles the exterior of the beautiful nave of Beverley Minster, and for simplicity and delicacy of design could hardly be surpassed. The bays are marked by plain aisle buttresses, terminating in three-cornered caps, with a battlement of cusped stonework ornamented with finials behind them. The buttresses of the nave are plain narrow bands of stone topped with small pinnacles. The roof is low pitched; the only other decoration is given by the uniform tracery of the windows and by a crocketed gable above each of the windows of the aisle.

North Transept.—The walls of the north transept are lower than those of the nave, and its roof, covered with a particularly ugly coating of zinc, is much more highly pitched. Thus the ridges of the two roofs are practically level, while the battlement of the transept is only on a level with the point at which the arches of the clerestory in the nave spring. The union of the two and the contrast between the low-pitched roof of the nave and the stilted roofs of the transept are rather awkward. It should be said that the zinc roof of the north transept was a necessity, as the old roof of stone tiles proved to be too heavy. But for these inevitable differences the

Photochrom Co. Ltd., Photo.]

THE EXTERIOR, FROM THE NORTH.

exterior of the north transept blends most successfully with that of the nave, though, of course, its details are altogether different. As an example of the great effect to be attained by the lancet windows, delicate proportions, and restrained ornament of the Early English style, it has never been surpassed. It extends three bays from the nave. The aisle buttresses end some little way below the battlements of the aisle. There are no buttresses against the main wall of the transept; but it is ornamented with a row of arches, some blank, and some pierced with the clerestory windows. These windows are in groups of three separated by two blank arches. The blank arches are wider than the windows. All the arches are decorated with dog-tooth mouldings. The absence of buttresses and the continuous row of arches cause a remarkable freedom from vertical lines in the exterior of the transepts, which is also characteristic of the interior. The battlements, both of the aisles and of the transept itself, are quite plain. The most admirable portion of this transept is its north front, which contains the famous group of lancet windows known as the "five sisters." These are five very narrow and long windows separated only by slender shafts. Below them is a blind arcade almost entirely without ornament, and above them another group of five lancet windows of different sizes, gradually diminishing from the central window to follow the outline of the gable. The details of these upper windows closely resemble those of the "five sisters," and they are flanked by two blind arches. The buttresses are also ornamented with blind arches, and appear never to have been finished, as they are truncated in an unusual way where one would expect pinnacles. The exterior of the western aisle of this transept is very curious in arrangement. There is an almost complete absence of division into bays. There are two lancet windows to each bay, and buttresses rise between them as well as between the bays. Thus there is nothing to mark the interior division of the main arches, clerestory, and triforium. All of these buttresses are cut short by caps a little way below the tops of the windows. Between the groups of aisle windows are blind arches narrower than the windows themselves. There is a blind arch of the same width at the southern extremity, and a wider one at the northern. The aisles,' like the rest of the transept, are almost perfectly plain.

The **Chapter-House** is connected with the eastern aisle of the transept by a vestibule projecting three bays beyond the north front. This vestibule then turns eastward for two bays, at which point it joins the chapter-house. Both vestibule and chapter-house are magnificent examples of Decorated work. Their date is doubtful, and is discussed in the history of the building. They are certainly among the finest works of Gothic architecture in Europe. The chapter-house is octagonal in shape, and is crowned by a lofty pyramidal roof. Its chief, almost its only decoration, is provided by the buttresses and the beautiful tracery of the acutely-pointed windows. The buttresses are of very curious design. They are joined to the wall of the chapter-house for nearly half their height, and up to this point are quite plain. They are then narrowed into lofty pinnacles, and these pinnacles are connected with the wall by two small flying buttresses, the lower one plainly moulded and sloping upwards to the wall, the upper one being horizontal and richly decorated with arcading, two arcades to each side of every buttress. At the point at which the buttress narrows into the pinnacle there are cusped gables with gargoyles on the outer side of the buttresses. The pinnacles are decorated with slender shafts and richly ornamented gables. The windows of the chapter-house contain five lights. They will be further described in the account of the interior of the building. Above them is a plain battlement, with two rows of ornament below it, and three figures in each bay above it. There is a very curious buttress at the point of junction of the vestibule and the chapter-house. It is joined to the wall of the chapter-house up to the battlement, and consists of an irregular mass of masonry ornamented as far as possible in the same manner as the other buttresses with gables and panelling. The two bays of the vestibule nearest to the chapter-house have nothing unusual about them except their buttresses. One of these is set close to the wall up to the spire of the pinnacle. All the other buttresses of the vestibule, except the one built against the buttress of the transept end, have pinnacles joined to the wall by a pierced arch of curious and ingenious design. The vestibule is crowned by plain battlements like that of the chapter-house, with small square-headed windows of two lights each. The windows of the two bays nearest the transept end are of most unusual design, which will be explained in the account of the interior; these bays are narrower than the others, that nearest to the transept being the narrowest of all.

The Choir.—The exterior of the north side of the choir is almost identical with that of the south; but there are some points of difference between the four earlier bays east of the transept and the four later ones west of it. In particular, in the four eastern bays the triforium passage runs outside instead of inside the building. The clerestory windows are recessed, and in front of them, running flush with the buttresses, is a screen of three divisions to each bay (see illustration, p. 62). The triforium passage, hidden by the roof of the aisle, runs below the screen and the windows, and between the two. The mullions dividing the screen run straight up to the battlement. The tops of the divisions are ornamented with cusped arches of open stonework. There is a transom crossing the mullions of the screen about one-third of the way up. It is difficult to say what was the object of this screen. It must have been included in the original design, and so cannot have been added afterwards to strengthen the walls. Whether it was a merely decorative experiment or an architectural device for the purpose of allowing the walls to be pierced with very large windows for the display of glass cannot now be decided. The effect from the outside is not good. The mullions break the surface into too many vertical lines, and, with the transom, take away from the dignity and purity of outline of the exterior. Inside, whether by a lucky chance or not, this screen, by darkening the clerestory windows, has greatly added to the effect of the wall of glass at the east end. There are also slight points of difference in the clerestory windows, showing the transitional character of those in the four eastern bays. The windows of the aisle are delicately moulded with capitals to their shafts, and are ornamented with a crocketed gable, ogge-shaped and topped with a prominent finial rising just above the battlements of the aisle. These battlements are pierced with cusped circles, below them is a cornice ornamented with foliage. The buttresses of the aisles are decorated with gargoyles and crowned with pinnacles of a considerable size with crocketed spires and finials. The front of these pinnacles is ornamented with characteristic Perpendicular panelling. The buttresses of the main wall are thin and plain, and, with the pinnacles, much resemble

BAY OF CHOIR—EXTERIOR.

those of the nave. The battlements are of pierced stonework of a common Perpendicular pattern. The eastern transepts do not project beyond the aisles. Their fronts contain very long windows of five lights, each with three transoms. The southern one has strong buttresses ornamented with panelling, and gargoyles at the corners. The northern is much plainer. Their side windows are like those of the clerestory. Britton conjectures that the unfinished state of the stonework on the north side of the choir beneath the window shows that a cloister or other low building was intended in this part, which was never executed. The cornice, he says, under the battlements is more perfect towards the western part and shows beautiful foliage. The spouts are sculptured with bold projecting figures through which the water is conveyed from the roofs.

The east end of the cathedral is square. The great east window of nine lights fills almost the whole of the central division. The buttresses separating it from the aisle are decorated with six storeys of niches, two to each storey, except the lowest, which contains only one. The east window has an ogee gable above it, topped by a curious pierced pinnacle at present in process of restoration. The ends, both of the aisles and of the choir itself, are square, and do not reveal the roof behind them. The arch of the great east window is surrounded with panelling, each panel curiously broken at different heights by cusped arches. The aisle windows have ogee gables above them with finials, and immediately above them a band of panelling running right across the exterior buttresses. These buttresses are large, and capped with lofty spires. The niches on them contained statues of Vavasour and Percy. Below the east window are the remains of sculpture representing Christ and His Apostles, Edward III. (on the north), and Archbishop Thoresby (on the south). These have suffered much in the frosts of recent winters. The square ends of both choir and aisles are decorated with arches with crocketed gables above them. Those of the south aisle differ from those of the north, being fewer in number and wider. All the niches on the east front except those mentioned have lost their statues.

There was certainly not very much opportunity for a fine architectural design in this east end with its great wall of glass, but, allowing for all disadvantages, it cannot be considered successful. There is no justification for the square ends concealing the roof. They are misrepresentations, and they are not beautiful. The decoration, with its monotonous rows of panelling and niches, shows the poverty of invention often characteristic of Perpendicular architects, and is sometimes positively ugly. The whole east front must surprise most people by its apparent smallness. It seems merely the end of an overgrown parish church, and not of a great cathedral, and though that apparent smallness is partly owing to the enormous size of the windows, which prevent any structural division of parts, it is increased by the monotony and shallowness of the decoration. It is almost impossible, in fact, to believe that this is the east end of the loftiest and widest choir in England. The buildings on the south side of the choir are the vestry, the treasury, and the record room.

The South Transept has a front entirely different from that of the north, though the sides are much the same. This front has three storeys of windows. Below, on each side of the porch, are two lancet windows. Above these are three more lancet windows, the central one of which, wider than the others, is divided by a mullion, probably a later insertion. These windows alternate with blind arches. On each side of the windows are slender shafts with capitals, and dog-tooth moulding runs round them and round the blank arches. Above these windows is a large rose window of "plate tracery"—tracery, that is to say, in its earlier form, in which the openings for the glass appear to have been cut out of the stone rather than the stone to have been added as a frame for the glass. This window is of a very elaborate design, and consists of three circles, the outer being the circumference of the window; the middle about equi-distant from the circumference and the centre, and connected with the circumference by pillars, twenty-four in all, and cusped arches; and the inner connected with the centre in the same way and ornamented with cusps. The spaces between the arches of the middle circle are pierced with trefoil holes, those between the outer arches are pierced and filled with glass. The outer circle is ornamented with three rows of dog-tooth moulding. Above this window, in the crown of the gable, is a small three-cornered window ornamented also with dog-tooth moulding. On either side of the rose window are small lancet windows with smaller blind arches on each side of them. Both windows and arches are surrounded also with dog-tooth moulding. An arcading with shafts and cusped arches runs along the base of the front, not quite reaching the exterior buttresses. In the centre is the porch by which entrance to the minster is generally obtained. It is reached by an ascent of two flights of steps. The porch is rather small, and not particularly remarkable architecturally. It consists of a single arch supported by an outer and inner group of clustered shafts. On each side of it is a small blind arch. All three of these arches are decorated with dog-tooth moulding. The interior of the porch is vaulted and decorated with blind arches. Above this porch are three blind arches surrounded with heavy gables, the middle and largest of which runs up to the lancet windows above it. It is difficult to believe that these arches and gables are not an addition later in date than the transept itself; they are so ugly and so meaningless, but they appear in the old prints of the minster, and the ancient clock, with two wooden statues in armour of the date of Henry VII., seems to have stood there from time immemorial. This clock was removed, with the statues, to make room for another at the beginning of this century, and it appears that the arches and gables were also altered, which may perhaps account for their present ugly appearance. The clock is now in the north transept. It should be stated that the whole of this front has been rather badly restored, and nearly all of its beauty of detail is gone. The aisle fronts have upper storeys ornamented with blind arches and an upper row of small lancet windows. These upper storeys do not correspond with the roof of the aisle behind them. The aisle windows are lancet, two to each aisle. The external buttresses are large, ornamented with gables and blind arches, and the other buttresses are of the same character.

Photochrom Co. Ltd., Photo.]
THE SOUTH TRANSEPT—PORCH.

On the whole, the front of the north transept, though very rich in ornament, is distinctly inferior to the front of the south. The rose window is too large for its lofty position, and its elaborate tracery and rich mouldings make it seem heavy. The lancet windows below it, being too long and badly spaced, have rather a bald look, increased by the richness of the rose

E

window above them, and the porch is altogether too insignificant and plain for its prominent position. But, as has been stated, the front has suffered much from restoration and later additions, and must not be too severely judged. When it was restored by Mr Street, pinnacles, which were late additions, were removed, and the present ones, more in keeping with the rest of the front, were put in their place.

The South Side of the Nave resembles the north in most respects, but the buttresses and pinnacles of the aisles are altogether different. The buttresses rise some way above the battlements of the aisles. They are plain to the level of these battlements, and above them are ornamented with niches containing figures, with blind arches above the niches. They are cut short by three gables, on the top of which are set lofty pinnacles. The niches vary in detail, some of them having more elaborate canopies than others. On these buttresses and on the wall of the nave are the marks of flying buttresses which have been removed, as has been stated in the account of the north side of the nave.

Three gargoyles spring from each buttress at the level of the battlement of the aisle. This side of the nave is only less beautiful than the other. The pinnacles, if they add to the richness of its decoration, break the simplicity of outline so admirable in the northern exterior of the nave. The stonework of the pinnacles and buttresses is much decayed, and constantly requires renewal.

The Central Tower rises a single storey above the ridge of the roof and is open inside to the top. But for small gables on the buttresses, it is quite plain up to the level of the roof ridge. Above this it contains two long and narrow Perpendicular windows on each side, of three lights each, with a transom. These windows are ornamented with ogee gables, and between them are three niches, one above the other, with canopies. The external buttresses are split up with vertical mouldings and ornamented with niches and panelling. The tower is crowned with a battlement. Horizontal string courses with gargoyles divide the buttresses at intervals. There are no pinnacles on these buttresses, and they appear never to have been finished. It is possible that it was intended to set another storey on the top of the present one, but this is merely conjecture.

This tower, or rather its Perpendicular casing, for it was

originally an Early English tower, is, with the western the latest part of the minster, but it is by no means the least beautiful. The English architects of the sixteenth century, if they were inferior to earlier builders in invention and vigour, were at any rate supreme in the management of towers. Their wonderful sense of proportion, their habitual use of vertical lines, and the character of their windows helped them to build what are perhaps the finest towers in Europe, and the central tower of York Minster is one of the finest of all. Even the absence of pinnacles, if it is an accident, seems to be a lucky accident, and gives this tower an unrivalled dignity and air of restraint suitable to the character of the whole cathedral. For whatever may be said against certain parts of the exterior, as a whole it is one of the most magnificent in the world. It shows best from certain points of view — from the north, for instance, or from the network of narrow streets to the south. It may be contended that the central tower is not quite lofty enough compared with the two western towers for perfect symmetry of outline; that, seen from certain aspects, it is rather square and box-like in appearance; that from no point of view are the western towers satisfactory. But the minster produces its great effect by its enormous bulk and dignity, its vast length, the variety and yet unity of its outlines, the severity and restraint of its form.

SEAL OF ST. MARY'S ABBEY.

CHAPTER IV

THE INTERIOR

The Nave.—The most casual observer will have noticed that churches of the Gothic style are divided vertically into bays, and that in cathedrals and large churches these bays are usually further divided horizontally into three compartments, the lowest consisting of the main arch and piers, the highest of a window or windows, known as the clerestory, and the middle, called the triforium, consisting usually of an arcade, sometimes blind, sometimes pierced, and occasionally even glazed. This triforium fills up the space between the top of the main arches and the bottom of the clerestory window which is covered on the outside by the roof of the aisle. As a distinct division or architectural feature, the triforium arcade is not a necessary part of the structure. In smaller churches it seldom exists. But in most cathedrals, as at York, a passage runs behind it, and is generally lit by the holes in the arcading. As has been stated, however, the arcading is often blank, and in such cases there might be nothing but a bare space of wall in its place, for all the practical purpose it serves. Since, therefore, its form is not dictated by considerations of utility, there is far more variety in its treatment than in that of the other two divisions, the main lines of which are formed by structural necessities; and yet the success or failure of an interior often depend upon the arrangement and proportion of the triforium; and the arrangement of the triforium, its emphasis or subordination, was one of the chief problems with which the builders of Gothic churches had to deal. Since such a church is generally divided into three storeys, the main lines of the interior would naturally be expected to be horizontal, and in many interiors of the Norman and Early English periods they are so, as, for instance, in the nave of Wells Cathedral. But the stone vault, which played so important a part in the

THE INTERIOR

development of Gothic style naturally emphasised, with its ribs converging at regular intervals, the vertical division into bays as opposed to the horizontal division into storeys. The supports of the outside wall were gradually concentrated by the use

Photochrom Co. Ltd., Photo.]
THE NAVE.

of pinnacles and flying buttresses placed between the windows; the windows themselves grew in size with the introduction and development of tracery and the increasing taste for the decoration of stained glass; until the final organism of Gothic architecture was attained, and the typical Gothic Church, from being a building of three storeys, pierced by windows, became a structure made up of vertical supports, with the intervening spaces filled with glass. When this phase of development was reached, the building became as organic in all its parts as the human body. Structure was ornament, and ornament structure, and the two were fused as they have never been in any other style of architecture. Decoration and variety of outline were supplied by the mere disposition of the supporting masses, the arrangement of structural lines; to the exterior, by the flying buttresses, the pinnacles, and the window tracery; to the interior, by the banded shafts, the capitals, the groined ribs of the vaults, and the openings of the triforium. Outside the church became a framework of glorified stone scaffolding; inside, an avenue of columns rising from the ground to the vaults, with intermediate spaces of tracery and coloured glass. But before this stage was reached there were many compromises and passing phases, and every considerable church in England, until the end of the fourteenth century, may be classified and criticised, not only for its beauty, but as a link in the development of Gothic architecture. The builders were grappling with both tendencies, the vertical and the horizontal; they were not consciously working on a theory of complete vertical development; they made progress by structural experiment, and a sensitive eye for possibilities of beauty; and in the meantime their problem, both structural and artistic, was to make a happy compromise between vertical and horizontal lines. It was a problem which probably presented itself to them in the question how they were to treat the different storeys of the building. Structural difficulties would be continually at war with their aesthetic ambitions, and the heavy stone vault made structural difficulties a serious matter. There was a growing desire for space, for height and width, for light and colour. With every increase of height and width the burden of the vault became more oppressive; with every enlargement of windows its supports were weakened. As a rule, the English builders were far less ambitious in their treatment of these problems than the French. Amiens Cathedral, begun at the beginning of the thirteenth century, is structurally as daring as can be. Salisbury, but for its spire, a later addition, is comparatively modest and timid. The French builders quickly reached the limits of structural possibilities, and their type became fixed. The English, with less economy of support, and a lower organisation of structure, were better able to play with their forms. So their churches present a series of continual and often inconsequent experiments in the treatment and proportion of every storey, particularly of the triforium, and in compromise between vertical and horizontal tendencies. Thus at Beverley, Salisbury, and particularly in the nave of Wells, the horizontal tendency is predominant, and the triforium is both important and continuous, without regard for the vertical division of the bays. In the Early English transept of the minster itself the triforium is the most prominent feature of the design. These are all examples of Early English work, but in the nave of Lichfield, which is Decorated, the triforium is still far more prominent than the clerestory. In the same way a various and experimental use may be noticed of the shafts dropping from the point at which the ribs converge. At Wells and Salisbury these shafts reach only to the top of the triforium. They are so insignificant as hardly even to suggest a vertical division. At Beverley they cease a little way above the capitals of the main piers, and are still very slender. At Exeter they are much more prominent, and terminate in rich corbels reaching to the capitals of the main piers; while in the later naves of Canterbury and Winchester, not only do they reach to the ground, but they are forced so far forward, and rendered so prominent by continuous mouldings on each side of them, that they become the most significant part of the whole structure. They seem to be the columns on which the vault is supported; and we have at last the avenue of stone.

The nave of York Minster was built at an intermediate stage, in which neither the vertical nor the horizontal tendency predominated. We might have expected, therefore, a design something like that in the naves of Exeter or Worcester; but the York builders were ambitious. They were determined to build a nave both lofty and wide, and with a great space for the display of stained glass. It seems likely, though we have no evidence to support the theory, that they were influenced by French example. There can be no doubt, as Professor Freeman has pointed out, that the design is more French than that of any other large

English church, hitherto built, except Westminster Abbey. The most casual observer will be struck at once by the large space occupied by the glass. The clerestory is unusually large; the main arches unusually high, and thus far the greater part of each bay is filled with the clerestory and the aisle windows. With so much space given to the highest and lowest storeys, it naturally follows that the triforium is almost squeezed out of existence. Indeed, out of a total height of 99 feet, there are only about 13 between the top of the main arches and the bottom of the clerestory. It would have been almost impossible to give so narrow a triforium a separate and independent design; and, therefore, by a device often found in French cathedrals, the triforium is merely a continuation of the mullions of the clerestory windows. Behind these mullions is the customary triforium passage; but the design really consists only of two parts, the clerestory and the main arches. It is as if the lower part of the light of the clerestory windows were divided from the rest by a transom, and pierced, but not glazed, so as to let in light to the passage behind them. This is the first example of this treatment, which was so happily followed in the naves of Winchester and Canterbury, in an English cathedral. In earlier examples, even where the triforium was decisively divided into bays and had ceased to be a continuous arcading, it was absolutely independent of the clerestory, as in the transepts of the minster. There can be no doubt that the plan adopted in the nave was a convenient and logical one. It is impossible to have every advantage; and where the designer has set his heart on a wall of glass, he cannot combine it with a rich and prominent triforium. Unfortunately, the architect of the nave, though ambitious and logical up to a certain point, did not carry his pursuit of the vertical tendency far enough. He aimed at unity and coherence in the design of each bay, and for the sake of that unity and coherence he was forced to sacrifice the richness and fulness of pattern given by a prominent and independent triforium. The later builders at Winchester and Canterbury made up for this, as has been said, by the emphasis they gave to their vertical lines. But at York, while the insignificance of the triforium deprives the design of all horizontal continuity, there is little attempt at vertical emphasis. True, large shafts rise from the floor to the converging point of the ribs of the vault; but these shafts are not forced forwards as at Winchester, but lie flat against the wall. They are prominent enough when each individual bay is examined, but they do not catch the eye when the nave is looked at as a whole. In the naves of Salisbury or Beverley the eye is led on from west to east by the circling band of the rich triforium; in the naves of Winchester and Canterbury it is attracted from floor to roof by the upspringing clusters of shafts; at York it wanders from point to point without any prominent feature to catch it. The blank space in each bay between the windows of the clerestory and the vaulting shafts ought to be a welcome contrast to the curves of tracery, the clusters of pillars and mouldings in a strong and forcible design. At York it appears to be simply a piece of wall which requires decoration.

Everywhere there is a lack of emphasis, not only in structure but in detail. The windows are not recessed, the capitals are small, the mouldings are delicate rather than forcible. The main piers are thin, their shafts are rather monotonously and tamely divided, the mouldings of the arches are narrow and shallow, the mullions of the clerestory and the shafts on each side of them are unusually slender; and this is peculiarly unfortunate in a nave, the width of which is greater both actually and proportionately, than that of any other English Gothic cathedral. To make a successful design of such proportions, there was need of strong vertical lines to give it the appearance of unusual strength: and not only the appearance but the reality. It is a significant fact that the builders were afraid to place a stone vault on their nave, and thus it is a Gothic building without that feature which gives its whole significance to the Gothic style, and by reason of which the design of this nave came to be what it was. It is a curious paradox, that the builders of York should have abandoned one of the most attractive features of earlier art in pursuit of a more logical design, and should then have been forced to abandon that very vault which gave their design all its logic. It is as if a dramatist strictly subordinated all his characters before the central figure of the hero, and then discovered that the exigencies of the plot would not allow of the introduction of the hero at all.

The most casual observer, on first entering the nave of York Minster, must have a vague feeling of disappointment, a consciousness that something is wanting; he will see that his feeling is justified, when he learns that it is the first building in

England of which the design is entirely dominated by the necessities of a stone vault, and yet that it is crowned by a wooden roof. But it must not be supposed that this nave is altogether to be condemned, as some critics have condemned it. Each bay, looked at by itself, is not only perfectly logical and coherent in design, but is filled with delicate and appropriate detail. The capitals, if small, are finely carved; the mouldings well contrasted and subordinated; and the window tracery is the finest possible. It is a work of the best age of architecture with all the characteristics in detail of that age; yet it is not the work of a builder of genius, but of a careful scholar, who has imperfectly assimilated the principles of his masters.

In passing this judgment, it must be remembered that we are not rashly coming to a conclusion on insufficient data. This nave is not a mere beautiful scaffolding deprived of all its original decoration, like the nave of Salisbury. If that is somewhat cold and wanting in richness, it is the fault of later ages, which have deprived it of its stained glass. At York the greater part of the stained glass remains. The vault has been renewed, it is true, but it can never have been satisfactory; and we may assume that in essentials we see the nave now as its designers intended us to see it.

To pass to a detailed description, the nave is divided into eight bays, of which the two nearest the lantern are narrower than the rest, no doubt with the purpose of giving increased support to the tower. It is about 263 feet long inside, and 48 feet wide, with the aisle 104 feet wide in all. Its height is about $99\frac{1}{2}$ feet. Each bay is divided into two main divisions of almost equal height; the upper half, consisting of the triforium and clerestory, being only about 2 feet longer than the lower, which consists of the main arches. These two halves are divided by a slender horizontal moulding running immediately above the crown of the main arches.

The piers of the main arches are octagonal in shape and unusually slender. They are made up of shafts of different sizes, the larger ones placed at the corners of the octagon, the smaller ones between them. The grouping of these shafts should be compared with that of the Early English piers in the transepts. There the central mass of masonry is surrounded with shafts of Purbeck marble almost detached. Here the different shafts are closely connected together and subordinated. The earlier pier is made up, so to speak, of a bundle of shafts; the later is a mass of masonry cut into different shapes. There can be no doubt that in this case the treatment of the earlier pier, if less logical, is more successful. The piers of the nave have capitals of beautiful design, and well executed, but rather small and shallow. The moulding of the arches is narrow, almost as narrow and small in detail as Perpendicular work, but, of course, much more diversified in outline. On each side of the main arches—that is to say, in their spandrels—is a series of shields with coats of arms, said to be those of benefactors of the minster. " Murray's Hand-book " gives the arms on the shields as follow, beginning at the north-east end of the nave:—

1. Semé of fleur-de-lis—Old France.
2. Six lions rampant—Ulphus.
3. On a chevron, three lions passant guardant—Cobham.
4. Barry of ten, an orle of martlets—Valence.
5. A bend, cottised, between six lions rampant—Bohun.
6. A fess, between six cross crosslets—Beauchamp.
7. Quarterly, in the first quarter a mullet—Vere.
8. A cross moliné—Paganel.
9. Barry of ten, three chaplets—Greystock.
10. Billetté, a lion rampant—Bulmer.
11.
12.
13. } Three water bougets—Roos.
14.
15.
16. } Five fusils in fess—Old Percy.

Beginning again at the south-west end of the nave the arms are:

17.
18. } Five fusils in fess—Old Percy.
19. Lion rampant—Mowbray.
20. Lion rampant—Percy.
21.
22. } Blank shields.
23. Two bars, in chief, three roundels—Wake.
24. A fess, in chief, three roundels—Colville.
25. On a bend, three cross crosslets—Manley.
26.
27. } A bend—Manley.
28. A fess dancette—Vavasour.
29. Three chevronelles—Clare.

30. A cross moliné—Paganel.
31. Three lions passant guardant, with a label of three points—Edward, Prince of Wales.
32. Three lions passant guardant—England.

At the centre of each pier rise three shafts to the point at which the ribs of the vaulting spring: a large shaft in the middle, with a smaller one on each side of it. There are small carved figures at the point at which the smaller of these shafts touch the moulding of the arches. The capitals of these shafts, though small, are of a very delicate design. A few inches above the top of the main arch is a horizontal string course or moulding dividing each bay into two storeys. As has been said, the triforium is merely a prolongation of the lights of the clerestory window. These lights are five in number. The division between clerestory and triforium is marked by a band of stone ornamented with quatrefoils. Below this is a cusped arch in each light of the triforium with a crocketed gable ending in a finial above it. The centre lights of the triforium in each bay originally contained figures, said to have been the patron saints of European nations. Of these there only remains a figure in the fourth bay from the west on the south side. Near the triforium in the opposite bay to this there projects the head of a dragon carved in wood, from which the covering of the font used to hang. The clerestory windows are of uniform pattern of the style known as geometrical Decorated. This pattern is very fine in design. It consists of five lights, the two outer of which are grouped in a single arch, with a quatrefoil piercing in its head. Between these two arches and on the top of the arch of the central light is a circle fitting into the arch of the window, and ornamented with four quatrefoils, four trefoil piercings, and other smaller lights. There are capitals to the outside shafts of the windows, and to the main shafts of the two inner mullions. All these mullions are very delicately moulded. A separate account will be given of the glass in these windows and those of the aisles, together with the rest of the glass in the minster. There is a curious moulding running round the arches of the windows and springing from the capitals of the vaulting shafts, which bends towards those arches to a point a little way above the capitals from which they spring, and then runs parallel and close to their mouldings. The vault is of wood covered with plaster. The ribs are elaborate in design, but not very successful. The fact that the vaulting is not of stone deprives the mouldings and bosses of all sharpness and delicacy. From the capital of the vaulting shafts and for about 9½ feet above them these ribs are of stone: the division between wood and stone is marked by a curious and heavy moulding. The aisles of the nave are bolder in design and altogether more satisfactory than the nave itself. Like the nave they are unusually wide and lofty. In the two farthest bays to the west, above which are the western towers, the rough wooden roof, which has never been covered with a vault, may be seen. These bays are separated from the bays next to them by strong arches with thick shafts and mouldings, which were built for the support of the towers. The shafts supporting this arch on the outer side are five in number. The shafts corresponding to them in the other bays of the aisle, to which the ribs of the aisle vaults converge, are only three. All these shafts have finely-carved capitals of leafage. The vault of the aisles is of stone, with only structural ribs, finely moulded and with carved bosses. The aisle windows are, like those of the clerestory, of the geometrical Decorated style, but of an earlier and simpler, uniform, design. They each contain

Photochrom Co. Ltd., Photo.]
SOUTH AISLE OF NAVE.

three lights, and there is no variation or subordination of mouldings in the mullions. Unlike the clerestory windows, they are somewhat deeply recessed. The mouldings of their arches are broad and bold, and are supported by five shafts with capitals. Above the three lights of the windows are three quatrefoils, pyramidally arranged. On each side of these windows, in the space between the windows and the vaulting shafts, is plain stone panelling terminating in an arch with a crocketed gable above it, ending in a finial which reaches to about the level of the spring of the window arch. On each side of this gable are grotesque carved figures. A small pinnacle is rather strangely inserted on each side of the arch at the point at which it springs. Below the windows there is a rich arcade, with buttresses between the divisions ending in pinnacles. Each division is filled with a geometrical pattern of two panels, each panel ending in a trefoil, with a circular trefoil in the head of each division, and a crocketed gable, terminating in a rich finial above it. All the mouldings of this arcade are very delicate. In the north aisle, and in the second bay from the west, is a doorway, which opened to a Chapel of the Holy Sepulchre, now altogether destroyed. Above this doorway is a gable ornamented with foliage and a statue of the Virgin, which has lost its head, with statues of angels on either side of her, also much mutilated.

The Interior of the West End of the Nave contains the famous window with tracery of the curvilinear or flowing Decorated style, and of a design only surpassed by the east window of Carlisle Cathedral. The glass in this window was given by Archbishop Melton, and is almost the finest in the cathedral. The tracery has been entirely and very carefully restored. The window contains eight lights. These lights are coupled in pairs by four arches with a quatrefoil in the head of each, and again formed in groups of four by an ogee arch above the other arches. The flowing curves of these ogee arches are most ingeniously and beautifully worked into the pattern of the upper part of the window, which contains five main divisions of stonework, each like the skeleton of a leaf in shape and in the delicacy of its pattern. Of these five divisions the top one is made by splitting up the central mullion; two diverge from it at the top of the lower lights; and two others curve inwards from the outside arch.

The central mullion runs up almost to the top of the arch. The mullions are alike in moulding and size. Below the window is the west door, the head of which is filled with ancient stained glass. There is a gable above it, running up to the bottom of the window and containing three niches. There are kneeling figures on each side of the gable, so that the top of it may have held a figure of Christ. All that portion of the west end not occupied by the window and the porch is filled with storeys of niches and arcading. The lowest storey consists of a rich arcading, each division of which is ornamented with geometrical tracery closely resembling that of the arcading of the aisles. These divisions are marked by pinnacles. Above this is another row of arcading of much the same character, except that it is about half as high again as the lower storey. Each division of this arcading contains two niches for statues, and above the niches are gables. Above the gables the divisions are filled with tracery closely resembling that of the lower arcade. This second arcade reaches to the bottom of the great window, which is marked by a string course running across the whole part. On each side of the gable of the porch is an extra niche rather clumsily fitted in. Above the string course the arcading is not so rich as below. The third storey consists of long niches ornamented merely with arches, gables, and pinnacles between each niche. The fourth is of much the same character, but that the divisions are shorter and have no gable above them. The last storey consists of plain panelling ornamented at intervals by gables. The west windows of the aisle are shorter than the other aisle windows, but have tracery of the same character. The aisle doorways are plain, but over both are some sculptured figures. Those over the north door appear to represent a hunt. In the middle a woman is setting a dog on to two beasts, and behind them there is a man blowing a horn. At the sides are two quatrefoils, set in which are figures (1) of a man attacking another man drinking, and (2) one man driving another away. The sculpture over the south door was destroyed in the fire of 1840, but a careful restoration of it has been made. It consists of a man in the middle fighting with a dragon, with sword and shield, and at the sides in the quatrefoils (1) Delilah cutting the hair of Samson, and Samson and the lion; (2) a man and woman fighting. The ends of the aisles are also ornamented with arcading in three storeys, the lowest of which is like the lowest storey of the arcading at the west end of the nave; the second a smaller series of niches ornamented with gables and pinnacles; and the third a single arcade on each side of the window, filled with geometrical tracery and resembling those on the sides of the other aisle windows.

It cannot be said that this mass of niches and arcading at the west end is either ingenious or successful. Arcading is a very beautiful decoration where it is employed, as in a triforium, in single storeys, to cover a definite even space. But where it is used to fill up an irregularly-shaped mass of wall which there is no need to decorate, it looks incoherent and confused. Had the wall been left bare it would have afforded an excellent contrast to the elaborate pattern of the central window. As it is, this decoration seems to be conceived in a spirit, of which there are further evidences in the decoration of the west front of the east end—the spirit of a builder determined to display the magnificence of his resources even at the expense of symmetry and refinement. This is a weakness that might be expected in the designer of a London hotel, but not in a great mediæval architect.

The nave was fitted with benches, seats, and a very mean-looking organ, in 1863. It is lit by gas jets round the capitals of the piers.

The tombs of the nave are described in a general account of the monuments of the church.

The present pavement dates from 1731. It was laid down according to the design of William Kent, under the direction of Lord Burlington, the amateur architect of Burlington House. The stone was given by Sir Edward Gascoigne from Huddlestone. Some of the gravestones were also used for the work. The work cost £2500, which was collected by subscription. The pavement, though inoffensive, is not in keeping with the rest of the church.

The Transepts.—The minster is generally entered by the door at the south end of the south transept, and this is perhaps an advantage, as it introduces the visitor at once to the finest view of the interior and one of the finest architectural views in the world.

Mr Fergusson has called the "lantern" the weak point in the system of Gothic, or rather of English Gothic, architecture (for in French churches there is usually no lantern), and there is something to be said for his view.

The climax of a domical church is obviously the dome. That is the centre and dominating feature of the whole design, and all the lines of the building should lead up to it. But in a Gothic interior the climax is at the east end. In the Middle Ages the high altar, blazing with jewels, plate, and costly embroidery, naturally drew all eyes to it. From the west end, therefore, the altar as a point of attraction was without a rival. But, as the visitor drew near to the transepts, the lantern, if it existed, suddenly discovered itself and distracted his attention from the altar. And when seen directly from below it had not the overpowering impressiveness of the dome. It was apt to be too narrow and dimly lit, too much disconnected from the system of the whole building to produce an overpowering and harmonious effect. But at York, when the minster is entered by the south transept, the east end is not seen at all, and the lantern, with all its height and vastness, is seen at once. Even as viewed from the west end, the choir is shut off from the rest of the church by a heavy screen, and the view eastward is broken and ineffective. But those very qualities of the interior which lessen the beauties of the nave increase the grandeur of the transept view. The great width of the church has enabled the lantern to be so large as almost to give it the effect of a dome. And the opening of the lantern is so lofty, 180 feet indeed from the floor to the vault, as to lessen the appearance of emptiness that might otherwise result from the great width of the transepts. The dimensions of this part of the church are all enormous, and only comparable to those of the dome and transepts of St. Paul's. The length of the transepts, each of them four bays long, is 223 feet from north to south, in itself the length of a large church; their width is 93 feet, the height to the summit of the roof, 99 feet, and to the top of the lantern, 180 feet.

The transepts, therefore, are unusually prominent, even for an English cathedral, and they have many other unusual features. Taken in conjunction with the lantern, they produce an effect to be found in no other Gothic church in the world. In England there are none so wide and so lofty. In France there are interiors even loftier, but in France the transepts are seldom a prominent feature of the design. Often they

F

do not project beyond the outer wall of the aisles of the nave, and oftener still there is no central tower large enough to allow of a lantern at all. It is a great piece of good fortune, also, that the five vast lancets of the north transept end, known as the five sisters, still keep their beautiful original glass. If we look at these windows and consider how utterly ineffective they would be if they were glazed with plain glass, we can understand how little remains of the original beauty of the interior of Salisbury.

When these transepts were planned, the minster had a Norman nave and choir, far narrower and smaller in every way than the present nave and choir. There is no doubt that the transepts were begun with the intention of rebuilding the whole church. At that time it was not among the largest of English cathedrals, and the aspiring and ambitious archbishops naturally desired to have a cathedral worthy of their position in the church. They therefore planned their transepts without any regard for the then existing proportions of the rest of the building, but as it was impossible to rebuild the whole minster at once, they found it necessary to fit their new transepts on to the older and smaller nave and choir, and afterwards to fit their new and larger nave and choir to these transepts. This necessity accounts for and explains many of the peculiarities of the transepts.

There is one peculiarity in particular, the arrangement of the bays nearest to the piers supporting the lantern, which must strike every observant visitor at once, and the explanation of which was only discovered by the patient and penetrating investigations of Professor Willis.

For the purpose of explaining this peculiarity of arrangement, the two bays of the west side of the south transept nearest the south-west pier supporting the lantern may be taken as an example.

It will be seen that their arrangement is most irregular—in fact, they can hardly be called bays at all. For instance, the main arch nearest to the pier is much wider than the main arch next to it, and this latter is filled with masonry. It will be noticed, also, that the pier between the two arches is Decorated in style, and not Early English, like the rest of the transept. Further, the triforium and clerestory do not accord in their division with the main arches. There is no triforium, but merely a blank

THE INTERIOR

space of wall with a small ornamental opening, next to the pier of the lantern; and this blank wall only covers a small part of the space over the arch below it. Near to the centre of that arch is a vaulting shaft, and south of it a full-sized division of the triforium, with a full-sized division of the clerestory above it, and the division fills the space above both the remaining half of the first arch and the whole of the smaller second arch. It is as if the *strata* of the building had been broken by a violent change, and this is exactly what happened. As has been said, the old Norman nave and choir had much narrower aisles than the present nave and choir; consequently, the bays of the transept nearest to the piers of the lantern were narrower than the other bays, so that their main arches might be exactly of the same size as the arches of the Norman aisles which at that point joined on to them. But when the far wider aisles of the present nave and choir were built these narrower arches did not fit them, and their outside piers blocked up the centre of the new aisles. The builders of the nave therefore determined to remove these piers and to alter the whole scheme of the arches, so as to make them fit the new aisles. By an extraordinary and daring feat of engineering skill, they were able to do so without disturbing the triforium and clerestory above them. This was effected in the following manner:—The pier in the middle of the new aisle was removed, together with the whole of the narrow arch which it supported on the one side and the wider arch which it supported on the other. No doubt, in the meantime the upper storeys of the two bays were kept from falling by temporary props. A pier in the Decorated style was then placed so that the arch above it fitted the arch of the new aisles, and the two arches—the narrower one nearest the pier of the lantern, and the wider one beyond it—were made to change places bodily, so that the same space was occupied by the two together as before, and it did not become necessary to disturb the rest of the piers. This narrower arch was then walled up to give support to the lantern. Meanwhile, of course, with this new arrangement, the upper storeys of the bays did not correspond with the arches below them. The narrower upper division was now over the wider lower arch, and *vice versa*. It should be said that the triforium of the division next to the piers of the lantern was built blank, because, being so much narrower than the other bays, it would have been impossible to give it decoration of the same character, and also because a solid space of blank wall would give better support to the tower. An account has been given in the history of the building of the minster and the manner in which the piers of the lantern gradually received their casings. The daring shown in this alteration of the transepts and the disregard for continuity of design are very characteristic of the builders of the period. They lavished extraordinary labour on beautiful detail, but they cared very little how one part of that detail fitted in with another. The spirit of their art was entirely opposed to that of the renaissance architects, for the success of whose designs uniformity and continuity of plan and detail were absolutely necessary. It is curious, also, that these very builders who were so daring and so profuse of ornament, were often very careless in matters of structure, and at times were even guilty of something very like jerry-building, as the account of the restoration of the south transept will show. The vaulting of the transepts is also most unusual and well worthy of attention. It raises many problems which have been little noticed by most investigators of the history of the minster.

Like the vault of the nave, it is of wood, and dates probably from the beginning of the fifteenth century. In the north transept it is covered with plaster; in the south this has been removed by Mr Street, and oak panelling inserted. It has been stated that the vault of the nave and choir, though wooden, resembles a stone vault in form and structure. Not so that of the transepts, which is a curious compromise between the form of the ordinary vault of stone and the simple barrel roof. It is an attempt, in fact, to combine the advantages of both.

It is the merit of groined vaulting that it emphasises the division into bays, and is capable of great richness of structural decoration. On the other hand, it involves a great loss of height, for the ridge of the vault can be little higher than the top of the clerestory windows, and it cuts off the whole space covered by the roof above it from the building which it covers. The structure of the vault will be perhaps most easily understood if it is conceived as a flat roof of stone of the same height as the top of the clerestory, supported by fan-shaped brackets springing from a point between the clerestory windows, and rising and spreading out until they reach the central ridge of the vault. As the vault is, but for these brackets, in its essence flat, there must of necessity be a great sacrifice of space between it and the roof above it. This sacrifice of space is obviated by the barrel roof, which nearly approaches to the shape of the outside roof, and fits into it without the loss of space entailed by the vault. But the barrel roof does not readily submit to a structural division into bays, or a structural decoration by means of ribs and bosses such as ornament and emphasise the divisions of the intersecting vault.

Wishing, as has been said, to combine the advantages of both forms, the designers of the transept roof have given it the shape of a barrel roof, and have covered it with a network of ribs, some of which converge between the bays of the building and meet at a point on a level with the bottom of the clerestory. The roof, therefore, has at first sight the appearance of a vault, but it remains a barrel roof divided by ribs all the same; and this will be evident so soon as it is remarked that the top of the roof is not on a level with the top of the clerestory, but some way above it. It is, therefore, not to be conceived as a flat roof supported by brackets, but as an almost circular roof ornamented and divided by structurally unnecessary ribs. Indeed, it would be altogether impossible to combine a vault with such a clerestory as is found in these transepts, for a vault is a roof designed to fit a pointed arch. Its spreading supports make it impossible to adapt it to any other than an arched clerestory; and the clerestory of these transepts, consisting as it does of a row of five lancet windows, is flat at the top. A barrel roof, on the contrary, will fit any kind of buildings, but, unfortunately, it is seldom successful, except in round-arched churches. To some of these—as, for example, in Auvergne—it has been applied with magnificent effect. It is very rare in England. It is always very difficult to decorate. The fifteenth century builders having for some reason or other decided on the form, and being but little accustomed to it, determined to treat it like a vault. They covered it with a network of ribs, and where these ribs met they placed bosses. They also caused these ribs, as far as possible, to take the same direction that the structure of a real vault would give to them. No doubt the ribs serve some useful purpose as a support to the roof, especially as that roof is slightly pointed and not circular, like the barrel roof proper; but the whole effect is unfortunate. The artistic merits of the real vault are evident. It is logical, capable of much structural decoration, and it determines and explains the whole plan of the bays both inside and out. The merits of the barrel roof are also evident. It also is logical, though in a less degree than the vault. It does not determine or explain the plan of the building below it, but it is easily adaptable, and it has a simplicity and a marked grandeur of its own. The roof at York has none of this simplicity. To the most casual visitor it is puzzling and complicated. To the eye which looks farther, which seeks for the logic of its construction, it is still more puzzling. It may deceive the careless observer with the idea that it is a vault, but it will not convince him that it is a good one. It is a work of great ingenuity, but not of great art. It is impossible to say what was there before it. If we knew, we might be able to understand why the builders of the fifteenth century hit upon such a form; and it may be that they were forced by structural necessities to do so. Some space may perhaps be allowed to a conjecture on the subject. It will be remembered that when the present transept was built no part of the present nave or choir was existing; and only the core of the piers supporting the present tower. The tower itself as we see it, the arches over the pier, and the casing of those piers, all date from a period later than the transepts. The Norman nave and choir, existing when these transepts were begun, were, of course, much less lofty than the present nave and choir. If, therefore, the roof of the transept was of its present height, it must also have been far higher than the roof of the then existing nave; and, consequently, of the four arches supporting the central tower, those to the north and south must have been very much higher than those to the east and west. If the transepts had had a vault originally, this arrangement would have been plainly impossible, as a vault would have covered up a great part of the east and west arches. But, though the shape of the clerestory makes it plain that a vault was never even intended, it seems very unlikely that the north and south arches were originally loftier than those east and west. If we suppose that they were all originally designed and built of the same height, we shall find a very plausible reason for the form which the present roof has taken. In such a case the transept must have had a flat wooden roof, the natural covering to a clerestory of such a design, and must have looked, with its great width, very squat and low. But when the new and far loftier nave was built, it, of course, became necessary to heighten the western of the four arches supporting the tower, and afterwards to go through the same process with regard to the eastern arch. At such a time, when the choir was completed, the two arches east and west would be much loftier than the two north and south. Before rebuilding the tower it would naturally occur to the builders to raise the north and south arches to a level with the others, and to do this it would be necessary to raise the roof. In such a case it would be quite natural for the builders to hit upon such a roof as at present exists. They would have before them already the example of a wooden vault in the nave, and for the sake of uniformity they would be inclined to make their new roof as much like that vault as possible. Having the size and height of their arch settled before they designed their roof, the roof would of necessity be shaped to fit the arch, and this would be the most convenient roof for the purpose under the circumstances. This theory will explain why a new roof was required in the fifteenth century, and it also helps to explain other difficulties. For example, it is hard to understand why the transepts, being so wide, are not loftier, and why their original design made a vault impossible. But if we remember that they were originally additions to a much lower nave and choir, we shall see that their architect, having determined on a plan of great width, was in a difficulty. If he made his transepts much higher than his nave, the effect, both inside and out, would be very irregular. If he made them of the same height, and vaulted them, they would be far too wide for their height. He therefore determined, we will suppose, to make a wooden roof which would sacrifice as little of the height of his transepts as possible, and yet allow them to fit on to his nave without any appearance of incongruity.

He may also have expected that a loftier nave would soon be built, and set a temporary roof on his transepts which could be easily removed and adapted to new requirements.

Be that as it may, the transepts are altogether a curious patchwork, yet when entered from the south end they seem almost entirely satisfactory, since the eye is so engrossed by the magnificence of the five great lancets of the north front, and the great height of the lantern, that it is unable to take note of any smaller and less satisfactory details.

The two transepts are alike in the arrangement of their bays and in the general lines of their design, though they differ wholly in the arrangement of their fronts, and in many little points of detail.

Their bays are planned on wholly different proportions to those of the nave and choir. There every bay is divided into two main divisions, and the main arch is nearly half of the whole. Here the divisions are three—a main arch, a very large triforium, and a smaller clerestory. The ornamental details are very rich and bold, but the design, taken as a whole, is not altogether excellent. Professor Freeman says bluntly that "the feeble clerestory and broad and sprawling triforium are unsatisfactory." This is true enough, but the whole effect is far better than might be expected. The great width of the transepts in proportion to their length, and the great size of the lantern, coupled with the fact that they are not vaulted, makes one apt to forget that they are divided into bays at all, and to regard the whole as a gigantic hall divided into three storeys and magnificently decorated.

The plan of the bays, like that of the decorated part of the choir at Ely and the nave of Lichfield, is probably a reminiscence of Norman proportions. It is certainly better suited to the bold outlines and masses of the Norman period.

Here, as in the nave, the main piers are rather thin. The triforium appears to be "sprawling," because it consists of a single great arch in each bay, sub-divided into four smaller ones. The clerestory is small rather than feeble. Its five lancets, though not large, are boldly decorated with shafts, carvings, and mouldings.

The chief drawback to the design lies in the exceeding prominence of the triforium, owing to which the eye is drawn to the middle storey, rather than led up from the floor to the roof. And as this middle storey consists of a single bold arch in each bay, it has not the merit of horizontal continuity, found, for example, in the triforium at Beverley, and does not lead the eye, once directed to it, from bay to bay.

Like the nave, therefore, though for very different reasons, the transept should be examined bay by bay if the beauties of plan and of detail are to be appreciated, and these beauties, at least those of detail, are abundant.

There are some differences of detail between the east and west sides of the south transept, and also between the south and north transepts. The east and west sides of the north transept are practically identical, except for the fact that a Decorated pillar without Purbeck marble shafts has replaced an original Early English pillar on the west side of the north transept. This was probably made necessary by the height of the tower.

The differences between the east and west sides of the south transept are as follow :—

The windows in the southern bay of the west aisle are blank. They are pierced on the eastern aisle.

The vaulting ribs of the western aisle are plain. They are elaborately moulded in the eastern aisle.

The arcade in the eastern aisle is shorter than in the western, and does not reach to the ground.

There is a niche against the north-west pier of the tower, but none on the north-east.

There is a leaf moulding above the clerestory on the eastern side. The same moulding on the west is plain.

The eastern moulding of the main arches on the eastern side is dog-tooth. It is plain on the west. The other mouldings of the main arches are also differently arranged.

The spandrels of the triforium are decorated with circles of carved foliage, five to each bay, on the west side. These are absent on the east.

The north transept differs from the south in the following respects :—

The arches of the arcade at the north end of the north transept are trefoiled. They are plain at the south end of the south.

The main piers of the north transept have a ridge running down their alternate stone shafts. This ridge is wanting in the south.

Their capitals are richer, and, curiously enough, apparently later in detail.

In the clerestory of the north transept there are large dog-tooth mouldings between the Purbeck marble shafts wanting in the south transept. There is also more dog-tooth in the arch mouldings of the clerestory of the north transept than of the south.

In the north transept the moulding between the clerestory and triforium is dog-tooth. It is plain in the south transept.

The arcades of the aisles are practically the same in both aisles, except for the differences noted between the east and west aisle of the south transepts.

There are two rows of dog-tooth moulding round the windows in the aisles of the north transept, but only one in the south.

The clerestory shafts in the aisle of the north transept are bolder than in the south, and the capitals, especially on the east side, are more elaborate and beautiful.

The extra Decorated pillar on the west side of the north transept has already been noted.

The ends of the transepts are, of course, entirely different in arrangement. Purbeck marble is used lavishly all over the transepts; as, for example, alternately with stone in the main piers, on the shafts of the aisles, and in the triforium and clerestory. The main vaulting shafts are altogether of Purbeck.

The arcade at both ends of the transepts is entirely without Purbeck marble.

In the south front the shafts of the lowest row of windows are alternately of Purbeck and stone. The arcading above the door is wholly Purbeck, with dog-tooth mouldings of stone. The shafts of the central windows are Purbeck with alternate dog-tooth mouldings, and there are Purbeck shafts at the side of the rose window.

There are also Purbeck shafts on each side of the door, beginning above the arcade below.

In the north front, the shafts of the five sisters and of the five lancets above them are alternately marble and stone.

As has been said, the proportions of the bays in the transepts are very different to those of the nave. The triforium is much larger, and the clerestory much smaller. The main arches, slightly smaller in proportion than those of the nave, are extraordinarily rich and beautiful in detail. Their mouldings are very complex and deep, and are varied with dog-tooth and billet ornament.

The piers are perhaps too thin, though beautiful enough in themselves. They are made up of alternate shafts of Purbeck marble and stone. Those of Purbeck are ringed half-way up. The Decorated piers are altogether of stone, and not ringed at all. The arrangement of the shafts is not quite so bold and various as in some other Early English work—the choirs of Ely and Worcester, for example.

The capitals are finely carved, though small. Those in the north transept are rather richer than those in the south.

The corbels of the vaulting shafts, which are placed just

Photochrom Co. Ltd., Photo.]
SOUTH TRANSEPT—TRIFORIUM AND CLERESTORY.

above the capitals of the piers, are very large and richly decorated with four rows of foliage.

They support three shafts each, one large and two very slender, as in the nave. On each side of the larger shaft is a dog-tooth moulding.

The main arches, especially on the east side of the south transept, are considerably out of plumb, owing to the great weight of the lantern, and perhaps to the inferior material used in the transepts.

The triforium consists of a single great circular arch in each bay. It is divided by a thick central cluster of shafts into two smaller arches, and these in turn are divided by slenderer piers into two smaller arches still. In the head of the largest arch is a cinquefoil opening ornamented with cusps and dog-tooth moulding.

In the heads of the smaller arches are quatrefoil openings decorated in the same way. The mouldings of the large arches are very bold, and ornamented with dog-tooth; those of the lesser arches are less bold and plainer.

The shafts of the triforium run down on to a gabled sill which cuts into their bases. There is the same arrangement in the choir.

The clerestory consists of an arcade of five divisions, the three middle being windows, the outer ones blind. The clusters of shafts dividing them are very rich and thick.

The mouldings of the arches are broad and deep, the dog-tooth ornament being profusely used. Above the arches is a cornice decorated with foliage.

The vaulting shafts terminate in the wooden ribs of the roof, without the division of a capital, about two feet above the string course.

The aisles are vaulted, as in the rest of the minster, with stone.

The shafts supporting the vault are very richly clustered and varied. The mouldings also are broad and deep; in fact, some of the finest work in the whole of the minster is to be found in these aisles. Below the aisle windows runs an arcade with trefoiled arches, which is very plain and simple in its details.

The ends of the transepts, as has been said, are altogether different. The arrangement of the windows of the south front is described in the account of the interior. That arrangement is not particularly happy on the outside. It is even less so when seen from within. This is partly the result of the stained glass of different periods now in the windows, and partly of the scattered and confused spacing of the windows themselves. Inside, as well as outside, the great rose window appears much too large for its position, and the vaulting, raised to allow the whole of it to be seen, fits awkwardly round it.

The north end of the transept, however, is one of the most triumphant successes in the whole minster. Its plan is magnificently simple. It is almost entirely filled by two rows of lancet windows, the five sisters, and five much smaller windows of graduated sizes above them.

The five sisters are, no doubt, the largest lancet windows in England, and it was a bold idea to fill almost the whole of that great front with them, but the boldness was entirely justified by the result.

It might perhaps have have been expected that, like other gigantic openings, they would dwarf the frame surrounding them. But this is not the case. They are enormous, and they appear enormous. They have an effect of gigantic and aspiring simplicity and vigour both inside and outside. They fill a given space in so obvious and efficient a manner, that it might seem that no other way of filling it could have occurred to the architect: that he was forced by a lucky chance to place them there. That, of course, is the greatest triumph of genius. It is a piece of luck however that they still retain their ancient glass—Early English glass of the simplest design, and of a beautiful silvery greyish green tint. Without it, no doubt, their effect would be entirely different.

The great size and height of the lantern has already been mentioned.

The wooden vault is covered with ribs elaborately reticulated.

There are two windows with simple Perpendicular tracery and transoms on each side. A single shaft runs between each window.

Below the windows there is an arcade of ten ogee arches on each side of the lantern, with pinnacles between. Above this arcade is a row of quatrefoils.

Below each division of the arcade are figures alternating with bosses of foliage.

In the spandrels of the main arches are coats of arms with angels above them.

The Chapter-House and **Vestibule.**—The vestibule leading to the chapter-house is entered at the north-east end of the north transept by a doorway of very curious design. It consists of two arched openings separated by a pier. Above the two arches is an acutely-pointed gable, within which, supported by the arches, is a circle with cinquefoil tracery. Above the gable is a further arch, the ribs of which join the gable at its exterior angles. This arch is further connected with the gable by a rib running horizontally through the crown of the gable, and below this rib, on each side of the gable, are circles quatrefoiled. From the finial at the top of the gable rise three ribs running to the top of the arch above.

It is impossible to understand the intention of this strange design, unless we suppose that the architect was determined to cover a certain blank space of wall at any cost. It is certainly an original effort, but it cannot be called either beautiful or logical.

The dates of the chapter-house and the vestibule are very doubtful. The question is discussed in the account of the building of the minster. It may be mentioned here, however, that the vestibule is later in date than the chapter-house itself.

The vestibule is a lofty and narrow passage running three bays north from the end of the transept, and then turning at right angles and running two bays east until it reaches the chapter-house itself. Just inside the vestibule will be seen the point at which the Early English work of the transept is interrupted by the Decorated work of the vestibule. There is no attempt at continuity. The Early English arcading breaks off just below the first Decorated window; the Early English shafts above it run close to the Decorated shafts of that window; while the Early English vaulting rib is cut off near its crown. It would appear from this that a passage to the chapter-house was begun and discontinued before the building of the chapter-house itself. The present vestibule was certainly built after the chapter-house, and the exterior parapet mouldings of the chapter-house may be seen within the vestibule, showing that it was almost an afterthought. Over the doorway leading into the vestibule is a pattern of blind tracery. Here, and on many portions of the roof and walls of the vestibule, are traces of old paintings. The windows are still filled with their magnificent original glass. The three bays running north are of unequal size, that nearest to the transept being the smallest, and that farthest away the largest.

The tracery of the two smaller windows is most curious and unusual. The smallest is also of a very odd shape, being almost as narrow as a lancet window, with, however, a rather obtuse arch. It is divided into two lights, which rise without further tracery to about three-quarters of the height of the whole window. Into the upper part are crowded five trefoils of different shapes, and piled one on the top of the other.

The mouldings of the shafts have a slenderness and delicacy characteristic of the whole of the choir and the vestibule. The slenderness is one of the chief arguments for the later date assigned to them. All the shafts have rich capitals. The next window is filled with even more curious tracery. It is divided into four lights, rising only to almost half the height of the whole window. The central mullion is thicker than the other two. Above these lights are two gables, to the crown of which the two side mullions run, through an arch below them. Above the gables are two more arches with trefoils in their heads, and in the crown of the window a circle cinquefoiled. The unusual feature of the design is the gables with the lights running through them. They were probably inserted to strengthen the wall. The next three windows are of splendid design, resembling that of the clerestory of the nave, but richer. All the mouldings are of the same character. Under the windows runs an arcade of blind tracery, two lights to each division, with a cinquefoil ornamented with a sculptured boss above. These bosses contain alternately foliage and human heads wreathed in foliage. The capitals are also ornamented with leaves and curious animals. The vault is of richly-moulded ribs, and on each side of these is a pattern of white lozenges on a red ground. The vestibule, as a whole, is one of the most beautiful parts of the minster, not less for its fine proportions and detail than for its magnificent stained glass.

The Chapter-House is entered by a doorway of most beautiful design, planned in the same manner as the western entrance of the cathedral, but plainer in decoration. It consists of a large arch divided into two smaller arches, each of which contains a door. In the head of the larger arch is a quatrefoil, at the bottom of which are two carved brackets for sculpture. Between the two smaller arches is a niche, with a canopy decorated with a double row of gables and finials. The niche contains a statue of the Virgin Mary and Infant Christ, so mutilated that little of their ancient beauty is left. Below this niche are four narrow shafts with capitals. On each side of the doors is a rich cluster of shafts, boldly cut and varied, with finely-carved capitals. The mouldings of the main arch and of the two subordinate arches are plain, but much thicker and bolder than those of the western doorway. On each side of the main arch are plain niches with small carved brackets. This doorway on the inner side is divided by a cluster of shafts, and above it is an oblong piece of masonry ornamented with arcading enclosed in an obtuse arch. Above the outer arches of the arcading, on each side, is a niche with sculpture.

The chapter-house itself is octagonal in form, being divided into eight bays. Seven of these are filled with windows, the eighth, that over the entrance, being ornamented with blank tracery of the same design as that of the windows. These windows are very acutely arched, and their tracery is of the geometrical Decorated style. They contain five lights, each light terminating in a trefoiled arch. The central light has further a very acute arch above it, also filled with a trefoil. The two outer lights on each side are joined together by an arch above them, in which is a cinquefoiled circle. Above are three circles arranged pyramidally, each containing nine cusps. The mullions enclosing the central light are thicker than the others. All the mullions are broken up into very slender shafts with capitals. It may be safely said that for elegance, symmetry, and the ingenious filling of a given space, the tracery of these windows is not surpassed in Europe.

Between the windows are clusters of shafts which support the ribs of the vault. These shafts have fine capitals, and are separated from the windows by blank spaces of wall set at an obtuse angle to the windows, so that the shafts are pushed forward. Below is an arcade, famous both for its richness and curiously beautiful design. It consists of a series of canopies, six to each bay, under each of which is a seat forming the half of an octagon. At each angle of these seats is a shaft of Purbeck marble. The seats, or niches, are divided from each other also by shafts of Purbeck marble. The use of Purbeck marble, both here and in the doorway of the chapter-house, is worthy of note. It is unusual after the Early English period, and might be advanced as an argument of the early date of the chapter-house. In the bay which contains the entrance, there is a seat on each side of the doorway. The capitals of the Purbeck marble shafts are carved with unusual richness; but it is the canopies which demand most attention. They are flat at the top, and each is divided into three bays in front, the central bay being divided from the other two by pendants richly carved with foliage of the same character as the capitals of the shafts. Between the shafts and the pendants are trefoil arches, one to each bay, and above the arches and pendants are gables crossing each other and ending in finials of carved oak leaves. Where the gables cross each other are carved heads and figures. The sculpture of the arcade as a whole is the finest in the cathedral, and some of the finest in England; but the art of the Gothic sculptor reaches its culmination in these heads. In grotesqueness, fertility of invention, and perfect fitness as decoration they could hardly be surpassed. The canopies

Photochrom Co. Ltd., Photo.]
CHAPTER-HOUSE—ENTRANCE AND SEDILIA.

are decorated at the top with a cornice of carved grapes and vine leaves. Above them is a passage running round the whole chapter-house and passing behind the vaulting shafts and through the masses of masonry between the windows. The vault is of wood, though ribbed and painted to give it the appearance of stone. This vault is arranged so that the ribs diverge from the vaulting shafts until they reach the central octagon of the roof. At this point they converge to the boss in the middle of the central octagon. This boss is modern. The roof was restored in 1845. Before this time it was painted with figures of kings and bishops, and the bosses were covered with silver. The modern decoration of the roof is dull and trivial in design and offensive in colour. During the same restoration many of the marble shafts were replaced and the floor was paved with tiles, with a most unfortunate effect. The east window has also been filled with very bad modern glass. In fact, restorers have done their worst to the chapter-house; but, luckily, their work is not irreparable. We may hope that some day the glass, the tiles, and the paint on the roof will all be removed. This chapter-house marks the farthest point reached in the development of such buildings. It differs from the chapter-houses at Lincoln, Salisbury, Westminster, and Wells in that it has no central pillar, and this absence of a central pillar is supposed to be its special glory. No doubt the pillar was an inconvenience when the chapter met, and the architect was given a fine opportunity for the display of his mechanical ingenuity when he decided to do without it. But there can be no doubt that a central pillar or cluster of shafts such as is found at Wells, would be more beautiful. And as the architect at York was afraid to vault his chapter-house with stone, his mechanical ingenuity was not put to so severe a test after all. And yet, though we may regret the beautiful central pillar as we find it at Wells or Lincoln, there are other respects in which this chapter-house surpasses all its rivals. In size, in richness of decoration, in boldness of outline, and in aerial lightness it is unequalled. Above all, it still contains six windows of magnificent stained glass. Even now it seems to justify its boastful inscription:

Ut Rosa flos florum, sic est Domus ista Domorum.

The Choir is separated from the rest of the church by a very elaborate rood screen, which was built *circa* 1475-1505, and is therefore the latest part of the original building. It is a fine example of Gothic work of the latest period, and though, the details are of course inferior to those of thirteenth century work, and the parts are small and rather crowded, the whole effect is one of great richness and magnificence. This screen consists of a central doorway into the choir, and of fifteen niches with rich canopies and bases, seven to the north, and eight to the south, of the central doorway. The niches are filled with statues of the Kings of England from William the Conqueror to Henry VI. The statue of Henry VI. alone is modern. It has been said that the original statue of this king was regarded with so much reverence as to have aroused the anger of the iconoclasts of the Reformation. At any rate, it was destroyed, and an image of James I. set in its place. This has been happily removed in the present century, and a statue of Henry VI., a fair work, by the hand of Michael Taylor, a local sculptor, has been inserted. The original statues are unusually good for their period, and it has been suggested that the details of their dress show some consideration for historical correctness. The same consideration was not given to the hair, for it has been pointed out that the Normans were clean-shaven and wore short hair, whereas the statues of the Norman kings have beards, moustaches, and long hair. The kings are dressed in robes of state. The legs of Stephen alone are exposed. The hands of the Conqueror are broken off. On the pedestals are the names of the kings, with the length of their reigns. They begin on the north side. The figures of angels above the canopies of the niches are made of plaster designed by Bernasconi, who also restored other parts of the screen.

The central archway is unusually rich and delicate for the period in which it was built. It is somewhat obtuse in form, and is surmounted by an ogee pediment or outer moulding. On each side are four narrow shafts with carved capitals, an unusual enrichment in this period. Between those shafts are rosettes and rows of foliage. The bases, both of the shafts, the pedestals, and the buttresses, are very long, as is usual in late Perpendicular work. The arch itself has four divisions of ornamented mouldings, with plain mouldings between them. The ogee moulding is richly decorated with foliage, and terminates in a lofty finial reaching to the top of the screen. Below this finial is an empty niche with a kind of ball-flower ornament at the base. On each side of this niche is an angel with a censer, with rich foliage below. The interior of the screen under the central arch is vaulted with carved bosses. The niches are divided from each other by buttresses decorated at intervals with pinnacles. The pedestals are long, and richly ornamented with tabernacle work. The greater part of the ornament of the screen is massed in the canopies. These canopies are made up of three inner arches, cusped, immediately above the heads of the kings, and five outer arches, cusped and gabled, round them. Round these outer arches is a mass of pinnacles, with three larger, richly-ornamented pinnacles, and two smaller, above them. Above these are three small figures, apparently playing on musical instruments, with other figures of the same size, one on each side of the buttresses. These figures, in their turn, have above them canopies of much the same character as those below. Above these canopies is a row of panelling with the plaster angels of Bernasconi above

Photochrom Co. Ltd., Photo.]
THE CHOIR SCREEN.

it, at the beginning of the cornice. The rest of the cornice is made up of a row of sculptured ornament and a row of cusped arches terminating in the "Tudor flower" ornament, alternating with rows of plain moulding.

The chief fault of this screen is its heaviness, which the mass of ornament is not bold enough in its parts to lighten. The central entrance is not cleverly managed, and seems cut out of the screen, as if to make a way into the choir at all costs. This screen should be compared to the beautiful rood screen at Exeter, with its three bold arches and its simple yet delicate

Photochrom Co. Ltd., Photo.]

THE CHOIR, LOOKING EAST.

THE INTERIOR

EASTERN BAY OF CHOIR—INTERIOR.

decoration. After the fire in 1829 it was proposed to remove it, and one is almost tempted to regret that it was not removed. The nave at York would be enormously improved by a closer connection with the choir. Under any circumstances the nave must be somewhat cold and ineffective; it would be far less so if the eye could pass with scarcely a break into the sumptuous choir. The naves of English cathedrals are too apt to look like splendid museums rather than places of worship, and this is peculiarly the case with the nave at York. Doctor Milner has stated, though apparently without authority, that this screen was taken from the Abbey Church of St. Mary, close to the cathedral. It is difficult to understand how it could have fitted so much narrower a building.

The choir itself, with the retro-choir or Lady Chapel, is divided into nine bays. It is considerably the largest and loftiest in England, being over 100 feet high and 99 wide. The altar is three bays from the east end, and one bay west of the altar are the eastern transepts. The choir was begun at the east end in 1361, and finished in 1405. There are differences between the earlier work east and the later work west of the transepts, which will be pointed out, though the plan of both is the same.

The plan, allowing for differences in detail caused by the change of style, is very like that of the nave. It is, therefore, an interesting example of a Perpendicular building carried out on the lines of an earlier Decorated design. When the east end of the choir was begun (1361) the Gothic style was fast reaching its fullest development in England. The nave of Winchester, a contemporary building, is the finest example of that development. There, as has been pointed out, the vertical division made by the vaulting shafts and the mouldings on each side of them becomes the most important feature in the design. The window tracery is planned merely as a frame for glass, and not as a design interesting in itself. Decoration supplied in earlier work by carved foliage, deep and various mouldings, and elaborate tracery, gives way to a system of lines emphasising construction as completely as possible. The contrasts between masses of ornament and blank walls, which play so great a part in earlier Gothic, disappear; and the only contrast is between the orderly lines of the stone and the kaleidoscopic decoration of the windows. Architecture loses much of its fancy and its delicacy, but becomes more logical, more reasonable, and more organic.

In the choir of the minster this change is only half carried out. There is a much greater emphasis of line than in the nave, and there is less delicacy of detail; but the vaulting shafts are no more important, and the window tracery still plays a considerable part in the design. Hence the choir lacks that air of decision, that extreme lucidity, to be found in the design of the nave at Winchester. If it were not for the choir furniture, the stalls, the throne and pulpit, and the altar, this want of decision in the design would be much more evident than it is. But the builders of this choir are not therefore to be blamed. They designed it as a choir, counting, no doubt, on the effect of the furniture, and as a choir it must be judged. It might have been expected, perhaps, that a building designed on the lines of the nave, but without the beauty of detail of an earlier age, would show all the faults of that nave and few of its beauties. But this is not the case. The architects were certainly most skilful; they had the immense advantage of seeing the design of the nave actually carried out, they understood its faults, and by a few dexterous alterations they produced a "fair copy" of it, avoiding most of those faults, and keeping all its structural merits.

As in the nave, the triforium is merely the continuation of the clerestory, the proportions, of the western bays at least, are almost the same as those of the nave, and the whole is covered again with a wooden vault, plastered and ribbed to look like stone; and yet that air of leanness, flatness, and emptiness, the chief fault of the nave, is almost entirely avoided.

A comparison of the differences in the two designs, and a demonstration of the small means by which the success of the later one is produced, must be both interesting and instructive, but, to be fully carried out, it would require more space than can be given in this book. We must confine ourselves, therefore, to pointing out some of the more obvious changes.

The most curious and important, perhaps, is to be found in the treatment of the triforium. In the earlier bays east of the eastern transept this treatment is the same in essentials as on the nave. That is to say, the triforium is on the same plane as the clerestory, and the triforium passage runs outside the building. But when the choir proper was begun, after an interval of some years, the architects, seeing, no doubt, that the older design was flat and somewhat wanting in relief, were seized by a happy idea. They set the clerestory windows some inches back, so that they were no longer level with the interior wall and with the triforium, and placed the triforium passage in its customary place. The difference in the design may be easily observed both inside and outside the building.

By this simple change, a greater relief and depth, a greater contrast of light and shade, was given to the whole design; and this without breaking its continuity or harmony in any degree.

The following differences in plan and detail between nave and choir may also be remarked:—

Besides the transom dividing clerestory from triforium to be found in the nave, there is a second transom in the choir crossing the openings of the triforium. This gives a greater fulness and complexity to the design.

In the eastern bays, below the openings of the triforium, the bases of the mullions are elongated to about two feet in length, and between them are cusped arches. These arches and the mullions themselves are set on a slanting ridge, like the mullions of the triforium in the transepts.

The vaulting shafts also do not terminate altogether at the point at which the ribs of the vault converge, but the outer ones rise some ten feet higher than the central one, until they are cut short by the spreading ribs of the vault. This is a difference characteristic of the Perpendicular style, which tends to an interweaving of lines, and an abolition of capitals, where possible.

The mouldings of the main arches also are broader than on the nave, and the clusters of the piers bolder.

It must also be remembered that, as the floor of the choir rises gradually to the east, the proportions of the eastward bays are materially altered, and the main arches are smaller relatively to the clerestory than in the nave. There is no doubt that this change is a fortunate one. It is also lucky that it occurs in that part of the building which otherwise differs least from the design of the nave.

Finally, it must be remembered, in accounting for the greater effectiveness of the later work, that a choir design is made for different conditions, and has different objects in view, from that of a nave.

It has often been remarked that the nave of York, examined bay by bay, is logical and satisfactory enough. It is only when it is regarded as a whole, and judged as an avenue of stone, that its faults are evident.

But the choir is not to be judged as an avenue of stone at all. It is cut in half by the altar. Its lower storey is concealed by the stalls, and its continuity broken by the eastern transepts.

In the nave, the lowest storey is the weakest. The thin pillars and the broad arches make too little division between the nave and the aisle. The whole is seen at a glance, and there is little of the mystery and shadow generally to be found in a large Gothic interior. Also the actual design of the pillars is poor. They do not fit well on to the arches above them. They seem almost insecure.

If these faults exist in the choir, they are concealed by the stalls, and east of the altar by the change in proportions. The

Photochrom Co. Ltd., Photo.

THE CHOIR, LOOKING WEST.

choir itself is like an enormous college chapel. The aisles exist, but play no part in the design, which still culminates in the splendid blaze of glass from the eastern transepts and the great east window, and once culminated on the still more splendid blaze of the altar.

The retro-choir, far too short and wide to be judged as an avenue of stone, is still more dependent for its effect on its glass. As most of that glass luckily remains, it is a miracle of airy splendour; one may see from it what were the objects, and how great the success of the much-maligned Perpendicular architects at their best.

It is still the custom to regard Perpendicular architects as altogether inferior to their predecessors; an opinion partly arising, no doubt, from Mr Ruskin's eloquent exposition of the principle that beauty of detail is the most vital and important part of architecture; and partly from the general idea that older work is always better than later. But Perpendicular artists were not altogether retrogressive. In some respects they adapted their design more completely to their material than the older men. Their woodwork, for instance, completely shook off the forms of stone. Their glass, in spite of all that has been said, is better decoration of a given space than the patterns of the Decorated period. This is particularly evident in the nave and choir of the minster, for the original glass remains on many of the windows practically undisturbed. The earlier glass is more delicate, and purer in colour. Its designs are often more interesting pictorially. Look at the window simply as an isolated example of stained glass, and you will certainly prefer the earlier work. Look at it as a patch in a whole system of decoration, and you will be inclined to prefer the later. The wonderful success, as decoration of fragments of ancient stained glass pieced together almost at random, goes to prove, almost as clearly as the pictorial errors of modern designers, that a stained glass window should be conceived, not as a picture, hardly even as a pattern, but as a simple arrangement of broken patches of colour. This is what the designers of the windows in the choir have done, for they have seen that by that means, and not by the representation of architectural forms, they obtain the best contrast with the real architectural forms of the building.

COMPARTMENT OF ANCIENT CHOIR STALLS.

At their best, the windows of the choir remind one of patches of coloured sunlight on running water. It is true that these windows are really filled with pictures, but these pictures are only an excuse and a stimulus for the inventions in pure colour of the designer. Without them his work might seem merely kaleidoscopic. It is his great merit that he has never allowed his representation of actual things to interfere with his decorative purpose.

To sum up, then, this choir has not the delicate and spiritual beauty of the choirs of Lincoln or Ely. That is never found even in the finest work of Perpendicular architects; but for stateliness and magnificence it has not a rival in England. These qualities may be best appreciated standing midway between the two transepts and in front of the altar. From that point glittering screens of glass and soaring shafts of stone are to be seen on all sides; the whole effect is one of triumphant light and space and colour, not to be surpassed by the splendours even of Moorish or Italian architecture.

To pass to a more detailed description: the original stalls were irretrievably ruined by the fire of 1829. An illustration of one of these stalls from Britton is here given. They appear to have been magnificent examples of Perpendicular woodwork, and their destruction is an irreparable loss. There were twenty of them on each side of the choir and twelve at the west end. The modern stalls erected in the thirties are a simple imitation, better perhaps than original work of the period would

THE INTERIOR

have been — better, certainly, than might have been expected—but spiritless in execution. The modern bishop's throne and pulpit are not even tolerable. They replaced a throne and pulpit erected in 1740, and, like the stalls, destroyed in the fire.

The fine Perpendicular altar screen was also destroyed by the fire. The present screen is a careful and very successful reproduction of it. It has been glazed with very good effect.

The reredos, designed by Street, with reliefs by Tinworth, is made of terra-cotta and wood, and is not successful either in colour or pattern. The carvings represent the first hour of the Crucifixion.

The clerestory windows are Perpendicular in style, and contain five lights. Though the design is not beautiful in itself, like that of the great east window, it makes an admirable frame for glass. There are certain differences in detail between the windows of the eastern bays and those of the western. The windows of the eastern bays are almost transitional. Certainly their Perpendicular character is not fully developed. Thus some of their upper compartments diverge to the left and right, whereas the windows in the choir itself are made up of parallel and vertical divisions. In the eastern windows, also, a transom runs through the upper lights of the windows, which is not found at the western. The tracery of the eastern window is even more filled with transitional characteristics. As a pattern of tracery, it is wanting in coherence and subordination, and these faults

COMPARTMENT OF ALTAR SCREEN.

are painfully evident outside. But it is so vast, and filled with such magnificent glass, that the tracery seen from the inside seems hardly more important than the leads of the glass, and the whole is to be judged simply as a great wall of glass supported where necessary by stonework made as unobtrusive as possible.

There are differences also in the eastern and western windows of the aisles, especially in the interweaving and subordination of the lines of the mouldings, but these differences are not so obvious as in the clerestory.

The change in the placing of the clerestory window and of the triforium passage has been pointed out.

Among other and minor differences the following may be remarked:—In the eastern bays the capitals of shafts in the triforium run round the shafts of the main arch of the window.

In the western bays the arches between the mullions of the triforium are cinquefoiled (they are trefoiled in the eastern bays), and the bases are much shorter.

All the mullions of the clerestory windows have capitals. The two central mullions, as in the nave, are thicker than the rest. They rise also to the head of the arch. The two outer lights are coupled by an arch above them. The upper lights are broken up into a number of divisions, vertical and parallel in the choir proper, slightly varied in direction in the retrochoir. The mouldings are as elaborate and as carefully subordinated as in the earlier work of the nave.

Below the transom dividing triforium from clerestory is a row of panelling divided by the mullions of the triforium, which, as in the nave, are merely a continuation of the mullions of the clerestory. The arches of the triforium are not ornamented with a gable, as in the nave, but with a moulding decorated with crockets and ending in a rich finial. The capitals of the main vaulting shafts are very curious. They consist of an ordinary row of carved foliage with three pendants ending in small carved figures with cinquefoiled arches between them. The outer mouldings of the main arches are cut short by the small outer vaulting shafts. A little way below them are small heads, as in the nave. The capitals of the main arches are like those of the nave, but their foliage is more disconnected. On the north side of the choir are figures on the capitals. Mr Browne, the enthusiastic and laborious historian of the minster, has supposed these figures to represent scenes in the rebellion in which Scrope took part. If the ordinary date given to the choir be accepted, it was built before that rebellion. But Mr Browne has endeavoured to prove that the choir was built later than is usually supposed. It is impossible in this book to do more than mention the controversy started by him, and to say that, in the opinion of Professor Willis and others, he has not made out his case. In the four eastern bays brackets and canopies for statues are attached to the vaulting shafts below the capitals of the piers. Those east of the altar were badly altered and restored after the fire of 1829. It should be mentioned two eastern bays are narrower than the rest for the better support of the eastern wall of glass, and the western bays for that of the tower. In the spandrels of the main arches are coats of arms, mainly of benefactors. The following is a list of these, taken from Murray's handbook to the minster, and beginning at the north-east end of the choir :—

1. Two keys in saltire—Chapter of York.
2. Six lions rampant—Ulphus.
3. Three lions passant guardant, a label of three points, each charged with three fleur-de-lis—Thomas, Duke of Lancaster.
4. Three lions passant guardant, a border—Edmund of Woodstock.
5. A bend between six lions rampant—Bohun.
6. Checky, a fess—Clifford.
7. A cross floré—Latimer.
8. Barry of ten, three chaplets—Greystock.
9. The instruments of the Passion.
10. Three estoiles of six points, a border—St. Wilfrid.
11. Two keys in saltire, a border engrailed—St. Peter.
12. Two swords in saltire, a border engrailed—St. Paul.
13. Seven lozenges conjoined, 3, 3, and 1—St. William. (Archbishop and Patron Saint.)
14. On a bend, a lion rampant—Musters.
15. A chief, three chevronelles interlaced in base—Fitz-Hugh.
16. On a saltire, a crescent—Neville.
17. } A fess dancette—Vavasour.
18. }

Those on the south side, beginning at the west end, are as follows :—

1. A cross—St. George.
2. A cross floré between five martlets—Edward the Confessor.
3. Three crowns, 2 and 1—King Edwin.

H

4. Barry of six, on a chief, two pallets between as many esquires based—Mortimer.
5. Six lions rampant, 3, 2, 1, with a horn on the west side of the shield (referring to the famous gift of lands)—Ulphus.
6. A lion rampant—Percy.
7. Quarterly, 1 and 4 a lion rampant for Percy, 2 and 3 three luces hauriant for Lucy—Percy.
8. A bend, a label—Scrope of Masham.
9. Six osier wands interlaced in cross—Bishop Skirlaw.
10. A bend, a border charged with mitres; over all a label—Archbishop Scrope.
11. Three water bougets—Roos.
12. A saltire—Neville.
13. On a cross five lions passant guardant—City of York.
14. Three fusils in fess—Montague.
15. A fess between six cross crosslets—Beauchamp.
16. A lion rampant—Percy.
17. France (ancient) and England (quarterly), with a label of three points—Edward, Prince of Wales.
18. France (ancient) and England (quarterly).

The vault of the choir is of wood, like that of the nave; it is an imitation of the vault destroyed by the fire of 1829. It is covered with a network of ribs that obscure the main structural lines of the vaulting.

The aisles of the choir are of much the same size, design, and proportion as those of the nave. Their vault is of stone. The windows are filled with tracery of an unusual transitional character, and altogether more beautiful and interesting than that of the clerestory. They are divided into three lights, each terminating in a very obtuse arch. Above these arches are three others, also obtuse and hardly pointed. Short mullions run from the points of the lower arches to the points of the upper. Above the upper arches are three irregular-shaped openings, arranged pyramidally, the two lower being quatrefoiled, the upper sexfoiled. The whole is a curious mixture of vertical and flowing lines. They represent a design, as it were, of which the tracery is arrested half-way in its process of stiffening from the curved lines of the Decorated style to the straight of the Perpendicular. Here, as in the clerestory, the mouldings are delicately varied. The central shafts alone of the mullions have capitals. On each side of every window are three shafts, all with capitals.

THE CHOIR IN 1810.

THE INTERIOR

Below the windows runs an arcade of very simple panelling, four divisions to each window, and two trefoiled arches in each division. There is also panelling of the same character on each side of the vaulting shafts between the windows. The windows of the eastern bays are more sharply pointed than the others. The vaulting shafts of the aisles have capitals of carved foliage and wings of leafage on a level with the top of the arcade below the windows. The windows next to the east end have only two lights.

The eastern transepts stand between the four western and the four eastern bays. They mark the position of the eastern transepts and towers in Roger's Norman choir, and are of rather unusual design. They are of only one bay in width, and do not extend beyond the aisle walls. They therefore represent a bay of the choir, of which the clerestory and triforium are removed, and the aisle roof is raised to the height of the roof of the choir itself. Both outside and inside their effect is magnificent. Their north and south walls are filled with enormous windows, containing splendid glass. Of these windows, that on the north contains scenes from the life of St. William, and is known as the St. William window; that on the south, scenes from the life of St. Cuthbert, and is known as the St. Cuthbert window. Both have had their mullions recently restored.

These windows are divided into five lights, and are crossed by three transoms. Below these transoms, in each light, are cinquefoiled arches. The upper lights closely resemble those of the clerestory in design, and are of the same size. The main arch in these transepts remains, and is of the same character as that of the other main arches. Above it in each case is a gallery with panelled openings. Above the main arch, on each side of the transept openings, are thick clusters of shafts. The lower part of the windows has double tracery, like the great east window, and the east windows in the Chapel of Nine Altars at Durham, the inner tracery consisting of open lights about a foot off the actual tracery, containing the glass, and of exactly the same design. On each side of the windows are five canopies and brackets. The arches east and west of the transepts and opening into the aisles are of the same character as those opening into the choir. Above them are windows of the same size and design as those of the clerestory.

In the spandrels of the arches are coats of arms as follow:—

North Transept—East Side.
1. A chief, three chevronelles interlaced in base—Fitz-Hugh.
2. A bend, a label of three points—Scrope of Masham.

North Side.
1. Three escallopes—Dacres.
2. A fess between six cross crosslets—Beauchamp.

West Side.
1. On a saltire, a martlet—Neville.
2. A bend—Scrope of Masham.

South Side.
1. Checky, a fess—Clifford.
2. A cross floré—Latimer.

South Transept—East Side.
1. A lion rampant—Mowbray.
2. A lion rampant—Percy.

West Side.
1. A fess dancette—Vavasour.
2. A blank shield.

North Side.
1. A fess between three cross crosslets—Beauchamp.
2. Three escallopes—Dacres.

The stone carving of the retro-choir, as the earlier work east of the transepts is generally called, was greatly injured by the fire. After the fire five of the canopies on the piers were renewed by the mason of the minster, who treated them according to his own sweet will. The canopies on the piers next to the altar screen remain untouched. The eastern bays of the aisles are of the same character as the rest. The east end of the choir is chiefly filled by the great east window, which fits into its position better than the west window of the nave, but not entirely satisfactorily. The mouldings of its arch are decorated with niches containing figures, and following the curve of the arch. This curve does not run parallel to that of the vault, which is less acute. The window itself is set back a little way from the wall, and on each side of it are mouldings with occasional niches. The outside mouldings of the window run straight up through the outside mouldings of the arch, and are cut short by the ribs of the vault. This interpenetration of mouldings is found also on the aisle side of the main piers of the choir, and is more characteristic of later German Gothic than of English. The wall between the outer mouldings of the window and the boundaries of the choir is filled with shallow niches, two rows to each side and four niches to each row. These perhaps were never meant to contain figures, and are more like panelling than niches. The upper outside niches on each side are cut into by the ribs of the vault. Below the east window is a row of quatrefoils, and below them nine divisions of panelling, in unequal portions, and of the same simple character as that in the aisles. The upper halves of the three central panels are filled with niches with rich canopies, each canopy being divided into three parts. The east end below the windows is now chiefly filled with uninteresting monuments of the later archbishops. There is no doubt that the aisles of the choir and the whole of the retro-choir could be better without the greater part of the monuments in them. The magnificent tomb of Archbishop Bowet is almost the only fine one to be found in the retro-choir.

There has been a considerable controversy about the position of the Lady Chapel founded by Archbishop Thoresby. This controversy, in which Mr Browne has endeavoured to prove that Thoresby's Lady Chapel was placed on the north side of the nave, is far too long and intricate a business to find a place in this book. It is enough to say that the other authorities seem unanimously to be of the opinion that the altar

THE VIRGIN AND CHILD—A CARVING BEHIND THE ALTAR AT THE EAST END.
Drawn by W. H. Lord.

of the Lady Chapel was under the great east window, where an altar, used for Holy Communion, is now placed. Thither, it is said, Thoresby removed the bodies of certain of his predecessors. And the tombs of six of these were existing in the seventeenth century, when drawings were made of them by Torre, the antiquary.

Brasses were placed over the burial-places of these archbishops, and were mostly destroyed in the Civil War.

The great east window, like the windows of the transepts, has a double plane of tracery reaching to about half the height of the whole. Between the two planes a passage runs at the base of the window, between two doors which lead to staircases in the turrets on each side of the windows. These staircases, in their turn, lead to a gallery across the window on the top of the inner plane of tracery. The view from this gallery is very fine. The window itself contains nine lights, and these are divided by two mullions, thicker than the rest, into sub-divisions of three lights each, each sub-division terminating in an arch formed by the curving of the mullions. From the top of each of these arches rises another mullion, the two outer being soon cut short by the arch of the window, the central one curiously splitting into two thick branches to right and left in straight lines until they also are cut short by the window arch. The rest of the upper lights are filled with an infinite number of small divisions, in which the occasional presence of curved lines shows the transitional character of the design. The window is crossed by three transoms, the two lower at equal distances, the upper close to the one below it. The gallery across the window is formed by these two upper transoms. The glass in the choir, as in all the rest of the church, is described in a separate chapter.

The entrance to the crypt is from the north aisle of the choir as it was in ancient days. There are still remains of the original vestibule to the crypt, and also the bases and one of the jambs of the Norman door leading to it.

The Crypt itself is very interesting, not only for its own sake, but for the light it throws on the history of the building of the minster. The fire of 1829 gave Professor Willis and Mr Browne the opportunity to make elaborate and prolonged investigations, to which we owe much of the light which has been thrown upon problems connected with the choirs of Thomas and Roger.

Before this fire, the only crypt whose existence was known of, was a small chamber under the platform of the high altar, no wider than the central aisle of the choir, and only equal to a bay and a half of that aisle in length. The greater part of this crypt was Norman in character. The vault was supported by six Norman pillars, and the ribs of the vault were apparently Norman. But the side piers were Perpendicular, and the transverse arches of the ribs four-centred, as in late Perpendicular work. There can be little doubt, Professor Willis says, that this crypt was a mere piece of patchwork put together, when the present choir was built, out of old materials which came readily to hand, with the object of giving support to the

THE CRYPT.

platform of the altar, and to provide chapels and altar room beneath it.

After the fire of 1829, the existence was discovered of a large crypt, stretching westward of the altar platform, and extending under the whole of the rest of the choir and its aisles. Of this crypt, only the pillars and the lower part of the walls remained.

At the west end of this crypt a portion had been enclosed in walls and filled up with earth. The eastern part was vaulted, and had stout Norman pillars at the side, while in the middle were two rows of smaller single pillars. The earth has since been removed, and the building laid open, repaired, and vaulted.

The thicker pillars are of elaborate late Norman work, diapered in a manner recalling the piers of the nave at Durham. The vault was ribbed. These pillars were, no doubt, erected by Roger Pont l'Evêque, and enable us to understand what the character of his choir must have been.

The walls enclosing the western part of the crypt are of peculiar interest. They are made up of three partitions. The outer wall, 3 feet 6 inches thick, is, no doubt, the work of Roger. The middle wall, 4 feet 8 inches thick, is faced with herring-bone work, and this, and the coarseness of its workmanship, prove it to be of great antiquity. It is almost undoubtedly Saxon, and has been supposed, though on slender evidence, to

CAPITALS IN CRYPT.

be part of the original church begun by Edwin in the seventh century. A bit of this wall is now bare, and may be seen.

The third wall is only 2 feet thick. It probably was also erected by Roger, but it is composed of older materials of an early Norman character. It may be from Thomas's choir, if, as is probable, the earlier choir which Roger pulled down had been built by Thomas. The stone of this wall is of the same coarse sandstone as the remains of Thomas's apse under the north transept, and there are traces of plaster on the stones showing that they had been used for the interior of a building.

No doubt the outer wall was erected by Roger as a support for his massive piers, for which purpose the middle wall alone would have been insufficient. Roger also probably added the thin inner wall, and filled the whole with earth, for the same purpose.

Close to the remains of the Norman doorway before mentioned, is a low arch, and the portion of an apse, no doubt the work of Thomas, the apse being the eastern termination of his transept.

It was from his examination of the side walls of this crypt that Professor Willis was able to support his conjectures as

CAPITALS IN CRYPT.

to the dimensions and character of Roger's choir. Thus he traced it to the eastern transept of that choir, in the same place as the present eastern transepts, and deduced from the extra thickness of the wall in that part that those transepts had been capped by towers. Beyond this the crypt was filled up with graves, and there is now no access, but during the repairs he was able to trace so much of the walls as to make it plain that Roger's choir had a square ending, and also to mark the situation of the east end of that choir.

The Record Room.—A chantry founded by Archbishop Zouch, but rebuilt in 1396, during the erection of the present choir, is now utilised as the record room, and contains the fabric rolls, and other documents concerning the building and constitution of the minster.

The vestry and treasury date from the middle of the fourteenth century; like the record room they lie to the south of the choir.

In the vestry is the famous horn of Alphus. It was given by Alph, or Alphus, son of Thorald, a little while before the Conquest. Alphus laid it on the altar of the minster, as a sign that he gave certain lands to the church. The horn is made out of an elephant's tusk. The wide end of the horn is ornamented with carvings of griffin dogs, a unicorn, and a lion eating a doe. This carving shows a strong Eastern or Byzantine influence, and may well have been of Byzantine workmanship. The horn was lost during the Civil War, but found by Lord Fairfax, who gave it back to the minster. The silver gilt chain now attached to it was added in 1675. The vestry also contains an oak chest finely carved with the stag of St. George, and dating from the early part of the fifteenth century, and the fine pastoral staff plundered from James Smyth, the Roman Bishop of Callipolis, in the streets of York at the time of the deposition of James II.

Here also is the Mazer Bowl or Indulgence Cup of Archbishop Scrope. It is of wood, with a silver rim, and three cherubs' heads for feet. Round the rim is the following inscription:—

"Recharde, Arche Beschope Scrope grantis on to alle tho that drinkis of this cope x dayis to pardune, Robart Gubsone, Beschope Musm grantis in same forme aforesaide x dayis to pardune, Robart Strensalle."

The cup was originally given to the Corpus Christi Guild, and afterwards passed to the Cordwainers Company. When the latter were dissolved (in 1808), the bowl was presented to the minster.

The vestry also contains three silver chalices and patens taken from the tombs of archbishops; the rings of Archbishops Greenfield, Sewall, and Bowet, also taken from their tombs; and an ancient chain, probably dating from the fifteenth century.

The minster, for all its size, age, and importance, contains curiously few tombs of interest. Though most of the earlier bishops were buried within its walls, not more than three of their monuments are really remarkable. Only one member of the royal family, William of Hatfield, the infant son of Edward III., lies there, and very few persons of distinction. It is not proposed therefore to give a description of any tombs, except such as are notable for beauty or interest.

Monuments in the Nave.—In the north aisle, three bays from the west end, is a monument of late Perpendicular work, said to be the tomb of Archbishop Roger, who died in 1181. It is possible that his bones were transferred here from the choir, though there is no record of such transference. This tomb was opened and restored in 1862, when some bones and remains of ecclesiastical vestments were found in it. The restoration appears to have been arbitrary and inaccurate.

EFFIGY OF MANLEY.

The tomb is recessed in the wall of the aisle, and consists of a lower storey for the coffin with a flat top, with a front of open stone work in eight divisions, each containing a quatrefoil. Above is a very obtuse arch with plain mouldings, with a row of "Tudor flower" ornaments on the top, and a figure of the Virgin in the middle. There are two birds holding scrolls in their beaks on either side of her. These have been changed by the ingenious restorers into eagles bearing ears of wheat.

All other monuments of importance in the nave were destroyed by the Puritans, or at the Reformation.

A word must be said, however, as to the tomb and shrine of St. William, the patron saint of the minster.

William Fitzherbert was a great-grandson of the Conqueror, and an opponent of the monks. He was expelled from his episcopacy in 1147, but returned to it in 1153. He is stated to have performed a miracle immediately on his return, and died about immediately afterwards in 1154. He is said to have been poisoned, whilst celebrating mass, out of the holy chalice itself. It was perhaps the peculiar atrocity of his end which gave him so great a reputation for sanctity. During his life he does not seem to have been distinguished above other archbishops for learning, piety, or good deeds. He was not canonised until 1284. It is difficult to understand either why the minster had not obtained a patron saint before this time, or why the choice eventually fell upon St. William. No doubt the authorities felt the want of a shrine fit to be enriched by the visitations of pilgrims, and were encouraged by the example of the shrine of St. Thomas of Canterbury to obtain one as soon as possible. We can only suppose that they chose St. William for want of a more distinguished patron. At all events, his shrine never obtained the celebrity of that of St. Thomas of Canterbury, and in after years was probably regarded as inferior in sanctity and interest even to that of Archbishop Scrope in the minster.

He had originally been buried in the nave, where, exactly, is not known, but it is said that even before his canonisation his tomb was visited by pilgrims, and was the occasion of miracles. When he was canonised, the 8th of June, the day of his death, was appointed for his festival.

The visit of Edward I. to York in 1283-4 was chosen by Archbishop Wickwaine as the occasion for the translation of St. William's relics from his old tomb in the nave to his shrine in the choir. The ceremony was performed with great pomp in the presence of the King and of his wife Eleanor. William became one of the King's patron saints, and Edward gave various gifts of jewels to his shrine.

In the Acta Sanctorum for June 8th, St. William's day, it is recorded that "Corpus ab imo in altum, a communi loco in chorum Venerabiliter est translatum."

"His body was translated with all reverence from the lowest to the highest place, from a common position to the choir."

The shrine was probably placed behind the high altar, and afterwards between the reredos and the eastern screen, as at Durham and St. Albans. The bones themselves were deposited in a portable *feretrum*, so that they might be easily carried in procession.

As in the case of Thomas à Becket, the original place of William's burial still remained an object of veneration.

It was at the eastern end of the nave, and was covered with

a great superstructure, so large that processions, it is said, were obliged to divide and march to each side of it.

The head appears to have been kept in a silver jewelled chest separate from the rest of the body. It was exhibited to worshippers who gave offerings to it. At the Reformation the head was seized by one Layton, afterwards Dean, and a follower of Thomas Cromwell; its seizure was one of the chief causes of the Pilgrimage of Grace.

At this time, also, the shrine was demolished, and also the superstructure over the saint's original place of burial in the nave. It is said that no remembrance was left of the spot except a tradition that the saint had lain under a long marble slab in the nave of the church.

In 1732, during the repairing of the nave of the minster, Drake, the historian of York, obtained leave to search under the said slab, and there found a coffin of stone, containing a leaden box, in which were bones wrapped in sarcenet. There was no inscription by which the remains could be identified, and they were again buried.

Archbishop Melton was buried near the font, as it then stood, at the west end of the minster. In 1736, when the new pavement was laid, the stone covering his grave was taken up, and a lead coffin was discovered, containing the bones of the archbishop. On the top of the coffin was a chalice and paten of silver-gilt. Inside the coffin was the pastoral staff, but no ring or vestments. The archbishop was re-buried in the same place.

Monuments in the South Transept.—In the eastern aisle is the tomb of Archbishop de Grey, who died in 1255. This, one of the two or three really fine monuments in the church, is Early English in style, and has been very little damaged. It consists of an effigy, with a canopy supported by nine pillars above it. The figure of the archbishop is clothed in full canonicals. In his left hand is a crozier, and his right is raised to bless. The feet trample on a dragon, into the mouth of which enters the butt end of the crozier. On each side of the figure is a shaft ornamented with bunches of leafage at regular intervals. Round the head of the archbishop is a gable cusped with censing angels on each side of it.

The pillars supporting the canopy have fine capitals, and

above them are cusped arches, with richly-carved scroll work in their spandrels. Above is a further tier of arches, supported by short shafts, also having beautiful capitals. Above these arches are gables covered with crockets, and on the gables are elaborate finials. These finials are an addition of the beginning of the century, and are of plaster. They are the work of an Italian sculptor, Bernasconi by name, and, considering the circumstances, are unusually good. Round the tomb is a railing, presented by Archbishop Markham, also of the beginning of the century, and of very poor design.

EFFIGY OF ARCHBISHOP DE GREY.

To the south of this tomb is the large and elaborate modern monument to Archdeacon Duncombe, which has nothing, either in workmanship or design, to recommend.

To the north is the tomb of Archbishop Sewall de Bovill, who succeeded Archbishop de Grey. His sepulchre, says Drake, was much frequented after his death by the common people, who reported many miracles to be done at it. The tomb consists of a plain slab of marble, with a cross upon it, supported by twelve low pillars, with plain capitals, and trefoiled arches.

Monuments in the North Transept.—In the eastern aisle of the north transept is the beautiful tomb of Archbishop Greenfield, who died in 1315. This tomb belongs to the most fully-developed period of the Decorated style. It is ornamented with arcading in front, with gables, each partition divided by buttresses with pinnacles. Above it is a canopy with a richly-foliated arch, and a gable with crockets, terminating in an elaborately-carved finial, with a statue of the archbishop in the act of benediction on the top. On each side are buttresses, with elaborate pinnacles. The statue of the archbishop is a modern addition. On the tomb itself are the remains of a brass. In 1735 this tomb was opened, and a ring discovered in it. Close to the tomb was the altar of St. Nicholas; and the archbishop was buried in this position because he died on the festival-day of that saint. This tomb is also remarkable for the fact that the lunatic Martin hid himself behind it, in 1829, before setting the minster on fire.

Near at hand, in the same aisle, is the tomb of Dr Beckwith (died 1843).

In the west aisle is a monument to Archbishop Vernon Harcourt (died 1847).

Behind the walled-up arch also in this aisle is a tomb, said to have been erected either to or by Thomas Huxey, who was treasurer of York from 1418 to 1424. Huxey himself, however, was buried to the south of the tomb. It consists of a slab, with the figure of a corpse below it inside a grating.

Monuments in the Choir.—We find here many monuments, but few of either beauty or interest. In the westernmost bay of the north aisle is the tomb of William of Hatfield, second son of Edward III., who died at the age of eight, in 1344.

MONUMENT OF WILLIAM OF HATFIELD.

The effigy of the prince is fine, though much damaged. Canon Raine has pointed out that the canopy is ornamented with the Plantagenista. The head was formerly supported by two angels, which have been destroyed (Britton). The feet rest against a lion. Drake relates that the vergers in his time asserted that this was the son of the Emperor Severus, buried at Acombe Hills, and carried thence to the cathedral. The statue appears to have been removed from its proper place, and neglected for a long time.

One bay east, and on the opposite side of the aisle, is the tomb of Archbishop Savage, who died in 1507. This is one of the latest of the Gothic works in the cathedral. It is a plain oblong, with four panels, containing coats of arms on each of the larger sides. It is surmounted by an effigy of the bishop, with mitre and crozier. Drake states that above it was a wooden chantry, of which there are now no traces. The name, *Thomas Dalby*, on the inscription on the tomb, is that of an archdeacon of Richmond, who is said to have erected the monument. Farther east, the outer wall of the aisle, as also of the southern aisle, is almost covered with pompous and ugly monuments, few of them remarkable either for their design or for the fame of the persons to whom they were erected. The best, perhaps, is that to Lionel Ingram, who died at the age of six. It is Jacobean in style, and has a pathetic Latin inscription setting forth the unusual virtues of the child.

The tomb of Archbishop Sterne, at the east end of the aisle (1683), is an example of almost everything that a monument should not be. West of this is the tomb of the unfortunate Scrope, beheaded by Henry IV. It is of little interest in itself, and was restored after the fire of 1829; but in the Middle Ages thousands of pilgrims flocked to it, and it was for a time more popular than the shrine of St. William himself. Henry IV. forbade offerings to be made to it, and gave these orders to the clerk of the cathedral.

"Y faces mettre sur la terre entre les pilers et par bonne espace de hors beilles fuystes et grosses piers de bonne hautesse et lacune iffint gils i soyent continuellement pour faire estoppoil a les faux foles que y beignont par couleur de devocion." The offerings were not, however, thus checked. Close by was the Chapel of St. Stephen, in which was the chantry of the *Scropes*, and so many offerings in memory of the archbishop were deposited there that it increased in riches up to the Reformation.

Farther west, between the aisle and the retro-choir, is the cenotaph of Archbishop Markham (died 1807), who was buried in Westminster Abbey.

To the north of the eastern altar is the tomb of Archbishop Rotherham, died 1500. It is a plain monument, Perpendicular in style. The top is a later addition; the whole was restored after the fire of 1829. The tomb was opened when a new pavement was laid in 1736, and a vault was discovered to run under it, in which were bones and a wooden head—" a piece of extraordinary sculpture for that age "—with a stick thrust into the neck to carry it on.

Under the east window are the tombs of Archbishops Frewen (died 1664), and Sharpe (1714), the latter being, perhaps, the ugliest and most absurd in the minster.

In a line with the monument to Rotherham is the effigy of Archbishop Matthew (died 1628). His tomb is on the south side of the retro-choir, and an unknown monument, with bases of pillars which once, no doubt, supported a canopy. This has been attributed to Sewall de Bovil, who, however, is buried in the south transept. Between the retro-choir and the south aisle is the beautiful tomb of Archbishop Bowet (died 1423). This is one of the finest Perpendicular monuments in the country, and far the finest in the minster. The stone which covered the grave was removed from it and used for the pavement in 1736, and the remains were laid bare, showing the archbishop's episcopal ring.

The canopy consists of an arch of a curious elliptical shape, over which are three clusters of tabernacle work, with pinnacles between them. The curious manner in which these clusters are joined to the arch beneath them, with fan tracery projecting outside the arch, should be noticed. The whole has been much destroyed.

At the east end of the south aisle of the choir stood the altar of All Saints, founded by Bowet.

A bay west of this is the tomb of Archbishop Matthew (died 1628), and north of it is that of Archbishop Musgrave (died 1860).

In the south aisle are the tombs of William Wentworth

son of the great Earl of Strafford (died 1695); Archbishop Lamplugh (died 1691); and Archbishop Matthew Hutton,

ARCHBISHOP BOWET'S MONUMENT.

(died 1757). All of them, like most of the other tombs in the choir, remarkable only for ugliness.

Stained Glass.—Undoubtedly the chief glory of the minster is its glass. There are 25,531 square feet of ancient stained glass in the church—at least twice as much, that is to say, as in any other English cathedral, and perhaps more than in any other church in the world. And this glass is of all periods. There are fragments of Norman in the five sisters and in some of the windows of the nave; Early English in the five sisters; Decorated in the nave, and Perpendicular in the choir. Further, the glass is almost all of very high quality—far higher, for instance, than that in King's College Chapel, Cambridge—and of infinite variety of effect. It ranges from the simple, almost uniform scheme of the five sisters, to the strong contrasts, definite forms, and glittering colours of the great west window.

It would require years of investigation and the writing of a large book to give an adequate description of this glass, and this has not yet been done. Facts, both as to its origin and subsequent history, are almost altogether wanting. As we see them to-day, the windows are in almost inextricable confusion. At some time or another, perhaps at the Reformation, or during the Civil Wars, the glass has been removed from its setting, and afterwards carelessly pieced together. It is now in the condition of a puzzle wrongly arranged. Outlines of figures have been filled with scraps of different colours, male heads fitted to female bodies, or inserted alone in incongruous surroundings, and glass of one period mixed with glass of another. Add to this that the glass was generally renewed and restored by one Peckett about 1780, who inserted patches and curious geometrical patterns of his own manufacture wherever possible, and an idea may be obtained of the difficulties which will beset anyone who tries to write an adequate book on the subject. It is only possible here to point out the main characteristics of the different windows and some of the chief points of interest about them.

The glass in the nave is mostly Decorated, with occasional Norman, Early English, and later insertions. Except in the three west windows, it is very fragmentary, and includes many of Peckett's additions.

The great west window is one of the most perfect in the church. It measures 56 feet by 25, and is almost entirely filled with its original glass, said to have been given by

Archbishop Melton in 1338. This is remarkable not only for the purity and boldness of its scheme of colours, but for the admirable way in which the design of the glass fits the elaborate pattern of the tracery. It will be noticed that both the figures and the architectural ornaments are in bolder relief than in the earlier glass of the five sisters, or the later of the choir. Some of the faces of the figures have been restored by Peckett, but not so as to interfere with the decorative effect of the whole. The window contains three rows of figures, the lowest a row of eight archbishops, the next a row of eight saints, including St. Peter, St. Paul, St. James, and St. Katharine, and above this a row of smaller figures unidentified. The window at the west end of the north aisle is also very fine. It contains a Virgin and child, and St. Katharine with her wheel. In one of the small lights above is a figure of St. Peter, crucified head downwards.

The kneeling figure below is obviously a later insertion, as may be seen from the incongruous colour of the arch above it.

The first window from the west in the north aisle of the nave is plain. The other windows are filled with fragments. In the third of these the top lights have been filled by Peckett, and contain the date of the insertion, 1779. The rest of these windows are free from Peckett's additions.

The second of these windows from the east is particularly worthy of attention. It is said to have been given by a guild of bell-founders. It was probably the particular gift of the Richard Tunnoc who died in 1330, after holding the office of Lord Mayor of York. Perhaps he was the head of the guild.

This window contains a most interesting representation of the casting of a bell, with an inscription, "Richard Tunnoc me fist," and also of Tunnoc kneeling and receiving the blessing of an archbishop, probably Melton. Above the figure of Tunnoc is the picture of a small window, and this certainly goes to prove that the window was given by Tunnoc himself. There are bells in the borders of the lights and other parts of the design.

The west window in the south aisle is as fine as its fellow in the north aisle. It contains a representation of the Crucifixion, in which the head of Christ is a later insertion, perhaps of the eighteenth century. The figure below, as in the corresponding window in the north aisle, is also of later date.

The first window from the west end is plain. The glass in the other windows is rather finer, and less fragmentary than in the north aisle.

The second window appears to have been largely restored. The tabernacle work is very crude in colour. It contains figures of St. Laurence, St. Christopher, another saint, and three coats of arms below. The top lights are fine, and perhaps of Perpendicular date.

The third window is one of the richest in colour in the minster, with its gorgeous arrangement of crimsons, greens, and blues. There are inscriptions by Peckett, with the date at the bottom, 1789. His deep blues on the top lights are particularly unfortunate.

The sixth window is also very bright. It probably contains Norman fragments. All the windows except the fifth contain insertions by Peckett.

The clerestory window contains fragments and coats of arms.

In the westernmost light of the second window from the west, on the north side, are portions of an Early English Jesse window. The wheel of this window, and those of the next five, also contain fragments of Early English glass. And in the lower lights of the fifth and seventh windows from the west are remains of the same date.

The wheels in the clerestory windows on the south side of the nave all contain Early English glass, except the third from the west. There is also some Early English glass in their lower lights.

The transepts contain less of their original glass than any other part of the minster. In the south transept there are fragments of Perpendicular glass in the east aisle, including figures of Michael, Gabriel, and St. William, and also Perpendicular fragments in the west aisle. The lowest row of windows at the south end of the transept has been filled with painted figures by Peckett, only better than the worst efforts of the Gothic revival. The figures represent Abraham, Solomon, Moses, and St. Peter. The glass in the five sisters, as has been said, is Early English of the simplest and most beautiful design. The colour, an almost uniform scheme of greyish green, is a curious contrast to the vivid blues and yellows of the period which preceded it, and examples of which may be seen in the choir of Canterbury. The pattern is an elaborate but restrained arrangement of the foliage of the Planta Benedicta (herb benet). The plain border surrounding the Early English glass was inserted in 1715. At the foot of the central light is a panel of Norman glass, the subject of which is either the dream of Jacob, or Daniel in the lion's den.

The glass in the west aisle of the north transept is modern, and of the worst character. A window by Mr Kempe in the east aisle is almost the only good example of modern glass in the minster.

The glass in the lancets above the five sisters is modern.

The glass in the choir is almost wholly Perpendicular. As in the nave, it is very fragmentary and disordered. The change in the character of the design will be easily noticed. The Perpendicular glass is not so clear and delicate in colour, and the architectural and other patterns are less pronounced. As has been said before, however, this glass, regarded simply as decorative, is perhaps superior even to that in the nave.

Mr Winton, to whom throughout in this short notice of the windows we are much indebted, has pointed out that the earliest Perpendicular glass in the choir is contained in the third window from the east in the south aisle; in the third and fourth windows from the east in the north clerestory; and in the fourth clerestory window from the east on the opposite side. These windows date from the close of the fourteenth century. There is also an early Perpendicular Jesse in the third window from the west in the south aisle of the choir. The other windows of the choir aisles east of the small eastern transepts, as well as the glass in the lancet windows on the east side of the great western transepts appear, he says, to be of the time of Henry IV.; the rest of the glass in the choir is of the reigns of Henry V. and VI., chiefly of the latter. He notices, also, that the white glass in the windows is generally less green in tint than usual, and that he has learnt from Mr Browne that it is all of English manufacture.

The great east window was glazed by John Thornton of Coventry. The terms of the contract for this work, dated 1405, are extant. They provide that Thornton shall "portray the said window with his own hand, and the histories, images, and other things to be painted on it." It was to be finished within three years. Glass, lead, and workmen were to be provided at the expense of the chapter, and Thornton was to receive 4s. a week, £5 a year, and £10 at completion, for his trouble.

The window is 78 feet high and 32 feet wide, and contains nine lights. It is entirely filled with old glass, except for certain pitches of modern glass, rather crude in colour, and inserted, it is said, after the fire of 1829. It contains 200 panels of figures. The subjects in the upper part are from the Old Testament, reaching from the creation of the world to the death of Absalom. The lower part contains illustrations from the Book of Revelations. In the lowest row of all are representations of kings and archbishops.

In the top lights are figures of prophets, saints and kings. At the apex of the window is a representation of the Saviour in Judgment.

This window is probably the finest example of Perpendicular glass in England. The windows in the south aisle are rather fragmentary. In the first two from the west the top lights are empty.

The second window is remarkable for the delicate modelling and drawing of the heads. The head of the Virgin reminds one of one of Lippo Lippi's Madonnas. That of an old man with a beard in the central light is German in character. If these are compared with the crude and simple design of the heads in the other windows, it will be obvious that they are of a different origin. Nothing, however, is known of their history.

The third window has borders by Peckett. It contains the Jesse noted before.

The fourth window is very fragmentary. It contains a beautiful figure of a saint in one of the top lights; the other top lights are by Peckett. In the central division, at the bottom, is the name of Archbishop Lamplugh, with a coat of arms. (Lamplugh's tomb is close to this window.)

The last of those windows contain painted glass given by Lord Carlisle in 1804, and bought from a church at Rouen. It is a representation of the Visitation, Mr Winton says, taken from a picture by Baroccio, and dates from the end of the sixteenth century. The upper lights contain the original glass.

The east window of this aisle is very fine in colouring, and fairly coherent in design. The subject is not clear.

In the north aisle the east window is also very fine. It contains a representation of the Crucifixion, with St. John,

THE EAST WINDOW.

St. James, and the Virgin. The first window from the east is very fragmentary.

The next three are among the finest in the minster. Their beautiful and unusual arrangement of greys, browns, and blues, should be particularly noticed. Their top lights are empty.

The other three windows contain paler, and less interesting glass; their top lights also are empty. The last of these was given by Archbishop Bowet.

The two great windows in the small north and south transepts contain scenes from the lives of St. William and St. Cuthbert respectively. They are 73 feet long by 16 feet wide. They have both been restored, but their glass is mostly original. The St. Cuthbert window was probably given by the will of Longley, Bishop of Durham, who died in 1437. It contains, beside subjects from the life of St. Cuthbert, figures of members of the house of Lancaster.

The glass in the clerestory is fragmentary, and contains restorations by Peckett.

The glass in the chapter-house and vestibule is chiefly decorated. There are, however, fragments of Norman and Early English glass in the upper lights of the vestibule windows. The glass in the chapter-house itself dates from the time of Edward II. and Edward III. The design is chiefly made up of medallions and shields. There are some modern restorations in the glass; and one of the windows—there is no difficulty in distinguishing it—is wholly modern. All the glass, excepting the unfortunate modern example, is of the finest quality.

CHAPTER V

THE ARCHBISHOPS OF YORK

Paulinus (627-633). The origin and even the nationality of Paulinus are unknown. It is said that he was sent from Italy by Gregory the Great to assist Augustine in Kent. Nennius states that Edwin of Northumbria was baptised by Rum, the son of Urien. It has been supposed that this Rum may have originally gone to Italy, and there taken the name of Paulinus, and that consequently Paulinus was a Briton; but this is mere conjecture. For over twenty years Paulinus remained with Augustine; but in 625 a marriage was arranged between Edwin, King of Northumbria and overlord of England, and Ethelberga, daughter of Ethelbert, the Christian King of Kent. Edwin, though still a Pagan, agreed that Ethelberga should be allowed the free exercise of her religion, and that she should bring a chaplain with her, who might preach the Christian faith when and where he chose.

The office was given to Paulinus, and before setting out he was consecrated Bishop of the Northumbrians by Archbishop Costus. For some little time Edwin remained Pagan, but he allowed his daughter to be baptised so soon as she was born. Finally, a conference took place between Paulinus and the nobles of Northumbria, probably at Londesborough, as a result of which Edwin, two of his children, and many of his court were baptised at York on Easter Day, 627; while the heathen high priest Coifi took the chief part in destroying a great temple at Godmandham.

But in 633 Edwin was killed in battle, and Paulinus fled with the Queen back to Kent. He was created Bishop of Rochester, where he remained until his death, 644. Afterwards he became the patron saint of Rochester.

633-664. After the flight of Paulinus the country relapsed into Paganism. When Oswald, a Christian, became King of Northumbria, he applied not to Canterbury but to Scotland for a missionary to his kingdom, and this was the beginning of the rivalry between the British and Roman churches in Northumbria. Aidan, a monk of Iona was sent, and became Bishop of Lindisfarne (635-657). He was succeeded by Finan (651-661); Colman (661-664); and Tuda (664-5). But these men cannot be accounted bishops of York. None of them received the pall, which, indeed, was given to no bishop of York between Paulinus and Egbert (735).

Ceadda and **Wilfrid** (664-678). Wilfrid, who had been educated in Italy, became Bishop of York, with jurisdiction over the whole of Northumbria. He refused, however, to be consecrated by a British prelate, and went to Gaul for that purpose. He was away three years, and, in his absence, Oswi, the King, appointed Ceadda (St. Chad) to the see. Ceadda was of the British Church, and was consecrated by the Bishop of Winchester. Wilfrid, when he returned, went to the monastery of Ripon, and lived there in retirement.

In 669 Ceadda retired, and Wilfrid became Bishop of York. Ceadda was made Bishop of Mercia.

Wilfrid did not obtain the pall, but exercised the powers of a Metropolitan. He restored the dilapidated cathedral, and built minsters at Hexham and Ripon.

He quarrelled in course of time with Egfrith, King of Northumbria, who induced Theodore, in 678, to divide his diocese into four bishoprics—York, Lindisfarne, Hexham, and Witherne. Wilfrid went to Rome to appeal to the Pope. His appeal was successful, but when he returned in 680 he was imprisoned, and afterwards banished. But in 686 Theodore intervened again, and reconciled him to the king. He was first given the sees of Lindisfarne and Hexham, and afterwards York, but he soon quarrelled with the king again, and left Northumbria. It is uncertain whether Wilfrid died in the possession of the see or not. He died, 711, aged 75. He was buried at Ripon. In 940 his bones were removed to Canterbury by Odo.

Bosa (678-705?) was educated under St. Hilda at Whitby. He retired in favour of Wilfrid in 686, but afterwards was reinstated. He was the first archbishop to be buried in the cathedral.

St. John of Beverley (705-718) was also a pupil of St. Hilda and of Theodore of Canterbury, who made him Bishop of Hexham, 687. The venerable Bede was his pupil, and speaks of many miracles which he performed. He enlarged the church at Beverley, and founded a monastery there. He was famous for his piety and good works. In 718 he resigned his see, and retired to Beverley, where he lived privately for about four years in his own foundation. He was buried in the church there. He was canonised in 1037, and his relics were translated and placed in a golden shrine.

Wilfrid II. (718-732) had been a pupil of St. John. He is said to have begun the dispute between York and Canterbury for precedence. Little else is known of him.

Egbert (732-766) was brother to Edbert, King of Northumberland, and, it is said, "by his own wisdom and the authority of the King, greatly amended the state of the Church in these parts." Gregory III. gave him the pall in 735, and he was acknowledged Metropolitan Archbishop in the north. He founded the famous school at York, where Alcuin was educated, and also the library.

Albert (766-782) had been a master at Egbert's school, and had greatly contributed to its renown. He also played a large part in the establishment of the library. He retired to the monastery at York, and died there, 782. He was succeeded by **Eanbald I.** (782-796), **Eanbald II.** (796-812), **Wulfsy** (812-831), **Wigmund** (837-854), **Wilfere** or **Wulfere** (854-890), **Ethelbald** (895), and **Redewald** or **Redward** (928).

Wulstan (928-956) was raised to the see by Athelstan, who was now King of England. He was imprisoned by Edred in 952, at Jedburgh, but was released soon after, and restored to his bishopric at Dorchester. He died two years after his release at Cundle in Northamptonshire, and was buried there. He was followed by **Oskytel** (956-972), and **Ethelwold** (972).

Oswald (972-992) had been made Bishop of Worcester in 961, and held that see, together with York.

After his elevation to the sees of Worcester and York, he became a great reformer of monasteries, and founded that of Ramsey in the Isle of Ely. He was a strong opponent of married clergy. He died suddenly at Worcester, after washing the feet of beggars, as was his custom. He was buried at Worcester, and miracles occurred at his tomb. He was afterwards canonised.

THE ARCHBISHOPS OF YORK 143

Adulf (992-1002) had been Abbot of Peterboro', and succeeded to both sees held by Oswald.

Wulstan (1002-1023) was also Bishop both of York and Worcester, but in 1016 one Leofsi was appointed his suffragan at Worcester. He died at York, but was buried at Ely, where there is said to have been a picture of him under the lantern.

Alfric Puttoc or **Pulta** (1023-1050) was Archbishop of York alone. He is said to have incited Hardicanute to set fire to the city of Worcester. He was a liberal benefactor of the church and college of Beverley, and built a magnificent shrine of the tomb of St. John. He died at Southwell, and was buried at Peterboro'.

Kinsi (1050-1060) had been a monk at Peterboro', and chaplain to Edward the Confessor.

Ealdred or **Aldred** (1060-1067). He was successively a monk at Winchester, Abbot of Tavistock, and Bishop of Worcester. He is said to have made his way by money and bribes to the see of York, with which he continued to hold Worcester. He had been much employed by Edward in diplomatic work. When created Archbishop of York, he went to Rome with the famous Tosti to obtain his pall. This the Pope refused, having heard, it is said, of his Simoniacal practices. But the Pope afterwards relented, on condition that he should resign the see of Worcester—this he did.

Once established as archbishop, Ealdred showed great activity as a builder and benefactor, especially at Southwell and Beverley. He also built a new cathedral at Gloucester.

He crowned Harold, and afterwards William. For this Drake calls him "a meer worldling and an odious time-server." He is said, however, to have exacted an oath from William that he would rule Normans and Saxons alike. Afterwards he excommunicated William for disregarding his oath, but William is said to have bought him off.

Hearing of the Danish invasion in 1069, he is said to have sickened at the news and died of a broken heart. Thus he escaped witnessing the vengeance exacted by William upon the north.

Thomas of Bayeux (1070-1100) was the chaplain of the Conqueror. He had assisted William with all his fortune in the invasion of England. In his time, the quarrel for precedence broke out with Canterbury. Thomas refused to make a profession of obedience to Lanfranc, and appealed to the Pope, and both went to Rome. The Pope, however, discreetly referred the matter back to the king, and at a synod held by William it was determined that Thomas should swear allegiance to Lanfranc, but not to his successors, and should be installed in Canterbury Cathedral; also that the Humber should be the southern boundary of his diocese, and that Worcester should be added to the see of Canterbury.

Thomas found his diocese in a miserable condition, owing both to the Danish invasion and the barbarities of the Conqueror. He rebuilt the minster, called back the frightened canons and made a provision for them. He appointed a dean, treasurer, precentor, and chancellor. He died at Ripon, and was buried at York.

Gerard (1101-1108) was translated from Hereford; he was a kinsman of the Conqueror. Like Thomas he refused to submit to Canterbury, and his consecration was delayed until he submitted at the command of the Pope.

Thomas (1108-1114) was the nephew of Thomas of Bayeux, and chaplain to Henry I. He also refused to acknowledge the supremacy of Anselm, and in consequence his consecration was delayed. Anselm dying, forbade any bishop to consecrate him until he had made his submission. At length Thomas submitted, and was consecrated by the Bishop of London. He died at Beverley, and was buried in the minster.

Thurstan (1114-1140) was the son of a prebendary of London, and chaplain to Henry I. Like his predecessors, but with more determination, he continued the quarrel with Canterbury. He refused to make his submission to Archbishop Ralph, who therefore refused to consecrate him. Thurstan was supported by three successive Popes, and was at length consecrated at Rheims by Calixtus II. Thus he alone succeeded in avoiding any submission to Canterbury. Henry I. taking the side of Ralph, deprived him of his lands, but the Pope issued a bull freeing him from all subjection to Canterbury, and threatened Henry with excommunication. In 1121 Thurstan returned triumphantly to York, and Henry submitted. The quarrel was revived by William de Corbeil, Ralph's successor, who was appointed papal legate as a compromise. Thurstan's victory over the Scots at the Battle of the Standard is perhaps his most famous achievement.

William Fitzherbert (St. William, 1143; deprived 1147, restored 1153-1154). On the death of Thurstan the see was not filled without a contest. The chapter chose Henry of Selby, Abbot of Fécamp, but the Pope refused his consent unless he would give up his monastery at Fécamp, and thereupon the choice fell upon William, who was a great grandson of the Conqueror. His election was not popular, especially among the monks. Accusations were made against him in Rome, where his election was bitterly opposed by St. Bernard and others. The Pope, however, agreed to allow his consecration, if the Dean of York would swear that his election had not been corruptly procured by the king. William was consecrated in 1143, at Winchester, and the pall sent to him in 1145. Meanwhile, Eugenius III. had become Pope, and fresh accusations were made against William, who went to Rome to meet them, but was suspended by the Pope, who, on hearing that certain followers of the archbishop had plundered the monastery of Fountains, deprived him altogether. (1147.)

Thereupon, **Henry Mordac** (1147-1153), the Abbot of Fountains, and like Thurstan, a friend of St. Bernard, was elected in his place. Stephen at first refused to receive him, but was induced to do so on the condition that the Pope would acknowledge Stephen's son heir to the throne of England. Mordac died at Beverley in 1153.

Meanwhile William had remained at Winchester. On Mordac's death he was re-elected. On his return to York, after it is said, performing a miracle, he died almost immediately, and so suddenly as to cause a report that he was poisoned at mass. He was buried in the cathedral, and pilgrims began to visit his tomb almost immediately after his death. Before long many wonderful cures were reported there, but it was not until one hundred and fifty years after his death that he was canonised. William is said to have performed thirty-six miracles after his death, and a list of them was once hung up in the vestry.

Roger de Pont l'Evêque (1154-1181) had been Archdeacon of Canterbury, and chaplain to Henry II. He was consecrated by Theobald of Canterbury, but without a profession of obedience. He is said to have instigated the murder of Becket. It was certainly after a conference with Roger that

Henry uttered the words which led to the death of the archbishop.

Roger also was the hero of the famous and ridiculous scene in 1176 at the Council of Westminster, when Robert of Canterbury having seated himself on the right of the papal legate, Roger, refusing to take an inferior seat, placed himself in Robert's lap. The unfortunate Roger was pulled off, beaten with sticks, and flung upon the ground.

Roger, however, was a good administrator, and charitable. He rebuilt the palace, and the choir of the minster, and also began a new minster at Ripon. After his death the king seized on his personalty. He was buried in the cathedral, and his tomb, though of much later date, is in the nave.

Geoffry (1191-1207), the illegitimate, and only faithful son of Henry II., was appointed only after ten years' interval, during which time the king took the revenues. He was early in life made Archdeacon, and then Bishop of Lincoln. He afterwards became Chancellor of England. He was only ordained priest when he obtained the archbishopric. He had sworn not to go to England while Richard was away on his crusade, but he returned immediately after his consecration at Rheims, and was clapped into prison at Dover. He was, however, soon released, and went at once to York. There he proved a better bishop than was expected, according to Stubbs, though Drake shrewdly remarks that "that author has made saints of every prelate he writes on." It is certain that he quarrelled always with John and Richard, or with the canons of York. At length he was suspended by the Pope, appealed, and was reinstated. Richard, on his return, seized all his goods, spiritual and temporal, but Geoffry obtained their return by payment of a sum of money. John also seized his goods, and Geoffry excommunicated all concerned in the seizure. He was from time to time reconciled with the king, but after a final rupture fled to Norway, where he died in 1212.

Walter de Grey (1216-1255) was only appointed after the see had been vacant for nine years, during which time John of course kept the revenues. The dean and chapter elected Simon Langton, brother of Stephen, Archbishop of Canterbury; but John would have none of him, and was supported by the Pope. Walter de Grey was therefore chosen at the desire of the king. He died just before the outbreak of the Barons' war.

He conferred many benefits on his diocese, and built the south transept of the minster, where is his beautiful tomb. He is said to have built the west front of Ripon Minster.

Sewal de Bovill (1256-1258) had been Dean of York. After the death of De Grey the see remained vacant for some time, the king saying that he had never held the archbishopric in his hands before, and was therefore in no hurry to let it slip out of them. He refused his consent to Sewal's election for some time, who, however, obtained a dispensation from Rome. He afterwards quarrelled with the Pope about the election to the deanery, and was excommunicated. This sentence lay heavy on the archbishop, and is said to have brought him to his grave. According to Stubbs, he began to "squeak" at last, and called for absolution on his death-bed. His tomb is in the south transept.

Geoffry of Ludham (1258-1265) had been that Dean of York over whom Sewal fell out with the Pope. When elected, he was still under the Pope's ban. He went to Rome, however, and by bribery and much trouble obtained his pall. Little is known of him except that in 1260 he laid the city of York under an interdict.

Walter Giffard (1266-1279) had been Bishop of Bath and Wells, and Lord Chancellor of England. He was with others entrusted with the regency of the kingdom during the absence of Edward I. in 1275.

William of Wickwaine (1279-1286) had been Chancellor of York. He died at Pontigny, and was buried there.

John le Romeyn or **Romanes** (1286-1296) was the son of that treasurer of York, an Italian, who had built the north transept and central tower of the minster. He had been precentor at Lincoln. He began the nave of the cathedral as it now stands. He died suddenly, near Burton.

Henry of Newark (1298-1299) had been Dean of York. Owing to the wars in Europe, he did not go to Rome, and was consecrated in his own church.

Thomas of Gorbridge (1300-1304) had been Chancellor of York. He was consecrated at Rome. He was said to be a great and learned divine. He was buried at Southwell.

William Greenfield (1306-1315) was related to Giffard,

a past archbishop, and had been Dean of Chichester, Chancellor of Durham, and Chancellor of England. He died at Cawood. His beautiful tomb is in the north transept of the minster.

William de Melton (1317-1340) was of lowly origin. He was elected in 1315, but not consecrated until two years after, owing to the interested delays of the Pope. He took a large part in civil affairs, especially in the war with the Scots, by whom he was defeated at Myton-on-Swale. His army was filled with clergy, and the battle was derisively known as the Chapter of Myton. In 1325 he became Lord Treasurer of England, and supported Edward in his troubles. He even intrigued against Edward III., it is said, in 1330, and was arrested for treason, but soon acquitted of the charge.

He completed the nave of the minster, and glazed the great west window. He died at Cawood. His grave in the north aisle of the nave was opened when the present pavement was laid down in 1736, and a chalice and paten taken from it.

William la Zouche (1342-1352) had been Dean of York. When Edward III. set out for the French wars he left Zouche warden of the northern parts of the kingdom, and as such he defeated the Scots at Neville's Crop, near Durham, 1364. He built, or began, a chantry on the south wall of the choir, which was destroyed by Thoresby. He died at Cawood, and was buried in the nave of the minster.

John of Thoresby (1352-1373) had been the King's Proctor at Rome, Master of the Rolls, Bishop of St. David's and Worcester, and Lord Chancellor of England. He drew up a famous catechism in Latin translated into English. In his time the controversy between York and Canterbury finally came to an end. The Archbishop of Canterbury was to be styled Primate of All England, the Archbishop of York, Primate of England. Each also was to be allowed to carry his cross erect in the province of the other.

In 1361 he began the present choir of the minster, contributing £200 a year to it during his life. He died at Bishopthorpe. It has been said that Urban VI. made him a cardinal, but this is probably not true. He was buried in his own Lady Chapel.

Alexander Neville (1374-1388) was a Canon of York, and high in the favour of Richard II. Consequently, on Richard's overthrow he was imprisoned in Rochester Castle, whence he escaped, and was translated to St. Andrews in 1386, but the Scots would have none of him, not acknowledging Urban as Pope. Thereupon, it is said, he fell to teaching a school at Louvain, where he died in 1392.

Thomas Fitzalan of Arundel (1388-1396), son of the Earl of Arundel, was translated to York from Ely, and had been Lord Chancellor. He was a great benefactor to the church and manors of the see, and gave much plate for the service of the minster. He was in 1390 translated to Canterbury, the first Archbishop of York to be so advanced.

Robert Waldby (1397-1398) had been an Augustinian friar and professor of theology at Toulouse. He was created Archbishop of Dublin and Bishop of Chichester before his translation to York. He died and was buried at Westminster.

Richard Scrope (1398-1405) was the son of Lord Chancellor Scrope, and was himself Lord Chancellor of England and Bishop of Lichfield. He received his perferment from Richard II., of whom he was a firm supporter, though for a short time he submitted to Henry IV. The history of his famous rebellion with the Percys, and the trick by which he was captured, is well known. He was taken to his own palace at Bishopthorpe, and there Gascoign, the famous Chief Justice, greatly to the king's wrath, refused to try him. He was condemned to death by a creature of the king, not even a judge, and beheaded near to York. He was buried in the minster, and was long lamented and almost worshipped by the people.

Henry Bowet (1407-1423). After Scrope's execution the see remained vacant for over two years. In the meantime, Thomas Longley, Dean of York, and Robert Halom or Hallam were nominated to the see, but, for different reasons, were not confirmed in the appointment. Bowet had been Bishop of Bath and Wells. He built a great hall to his castle at Cawood, where he died, and was buried in the east end of the cathedral, near the altar of All Saints, which he had built. His beautiful tomb may still be seen.

John Kemp (1426-1452) had been Bishop of Rochester, Chichester, and London. He was the nominee of the king and the dean and chapter, as opposed to the Pope, who proposed Fleming, Bishop of London. The Pope, whose power was fast decaying in England, at length submitted. Kemp, who was, it is said, of humble birth, rose to be Cardinal, first of St. Balbria, and afterwards of St. Rupria. He was translated finally to Canterbury.

In 1432 he went as ambassador to the Council of Bâle. He built a gatehouse to the palace at Cawood. He died soon after his translation to Canterbury.

William Booth or **Bothe** (1452-1464) had been a lawyer, and Bishop of Lichfield. He repaired the palaces at Southwell and York, and died at Southwell, where he was buried.

George Neville (1464-1476), by the interest of his brother Warwick, the king-maker, became Bishop of Exeter at the age of twenty-three. He was not thirty when made archbishop. His installation was the most splendid ceremony of the kind hitherto seen, but his tenure of the see was marked by many troubles. When Edward IV. was captured by Warwick at Oundle he was given into the custody of the archbishop, who treated him with great courtesy and freedom, so that he soon escaped to London. Soon after Edward captured the archbishop and imprisoned him; but soon released him and restored him to his see. Again he was arrested for high treason and sent to Calais, the king having plundered all his plate and jewels. He was imprisoned for four years, and died soon after his release. His tomb was unknown, but Drake speaks of a grave found under the Dean's vestry about 1735, which, from its contents, must have been that of an archbishop, and perhaps of Neville.

Laurence Booth or **Bothe** (1476-1480) had been Bishop of Durham and Lord High Chancellor; he died at Southwell, and was buried there.

Thomas Scott or **de Rotheram** (1480-1500) had been Bishop of Rochester and Lincoln, and Lord High Chancellor. He was imprisoned in the Tower by Richard III., for delivering up the Great Seal to the Queen on the death of Edward IV., but was soon released. He completed Lincoln College, Oxford, and gave a "wonderful rich mitre" to the minster. He was buried in the Lady Chapel, where his tomb still remains.

Thomas Savage (1501-1507) had been Bishop of Rochester and London. He was nominated by the king, confirmed by the Pope, and installed by deputy. He was buried on the north-west side of the choir, where his tomb remains.

Christopher Baynbridge (1508-1514) had been Dean of York, Dean of Windsor, Master of the Rolls, and Bishop of Durham. In 1511 he became Cardinal of St. Praxede. He was sent by Henry VIII. to the court of the Pope as King's Proctor. There he died, poisoned by a servant. He was buried at Rome, in the church of St. Thomas the Martyr.

Thomas Wolsey (1514-1530). The facts of the life of this famous man are too well known to need repetition. He was at once Bishop of Durham and Archbishop of York, and afterwards Bishop of Winchester and Archbishop of York. In 1515 he was created Cardinal of St. Cecilia, and papal legate. It is said that Wolsey never was at York, though he was arrested at Cawood after his disgrace.

Edward Lee (1531-1544). The king delayed a year before he appointed Edward Lee, his almoner, to the vacant see. In 1536, when the Pilgrimage of Grace broke out, he was seized by the rebels and carried to Pontefract Castle, where he was compelled to take an oath that he would support the rebel party. His tomb is in the choir.

EFFIGY OF ARCHBISHOP SAVAGE.

Robert Holgate (1545-1554) was translated from Landaff. He supported Henry in the Reformation. He was even married. When Mary came to the throne his wife and his riches were taken from him, and himself cast into the Tower. After a year and a half's imprisonment he was released, and died soon after at Hemsworth.

Nicholas Heath (1555-1559) had been Bishop of Landaff, Rochester, and Worcester, and, under Mary, Lord President of

TOMB OF ARCHBISHOP SAVAGE.

Wales and Lord Chancellor. The Bull of Pope Paul IV. appointing him to York is the last acknowledged in England. He obtained much of the property from the Queen which Henry VIII. had alienated from the see. On the accession of Elizabeth, Heath was deprived, though he had proclaimed her Queen. He retired to Cobham in Surrey. The queen appears to have punished him only for his opinions, since he remained a firm Papist. Elizabeth even visited him at Cobham. He died in 1579.

THE ARCHBISHOPS OF YORK

Thomas Young (1561-1568) had been Bishop of St. David's, and was president of the Council of the North. It is said he provided for his family by settling the best estates of the prebends upon them. Late in life he married, and, it is said, pulled down the great hall in the palace at York that he might give the lead to his son. He died at Sheffield Manor.

Edward Grindal (1570-1576) had been Bishop of London. He was a Puritan, and afterwards was translated to Canterbury.

Edwin Sandys (1577-1588), when vice-chancellor of Cambridge University, supported the cause of Lady Jane Grey. For this he was thrown into prison, and afterwards fled to Germany. He returned on the accession of Elizabeth, and was made Bishop of Worcester, and afterwards of London. He died at Southwell, where he was buried.

John Piers (1588-1594) had been Dean of Christchurch, Oxford, Bishop of Rochester, and Bishop of Salisbury.

Matthew Hutton (1595-1606) was translated from Durham. His monument is in the south aisle of the choir.

Tobias Matthew (1606-1628) was also translated from Durham. His monument is in the south aisle of the choir.

George Monteign (1628) had been Bishop of Lincoln, London, and Durham. He died within a month of his enthronement.

Samuel Hursnett (1628-1631) was translated from Norwich. He had been master of Pembroke Hall, Cambridge, where he was ejected for scandalous practices. He died unmarried, and on his tomb described himself as *Indignus Episcopus Cicestriensis, indignior norvicencis, indignissimus Archiepiscopus Eboracensis.*

Richard Neile (1632-1640) was Dean of Westminster in 1605. Lord Burghley was his patron, and he became Bishop of Rochester, Lichfield, Lincoln, Durham, and Winchester; more sees than any other English bishop has ruled over. He was a supporter of Laud, and a courtier. He died in 1640.

John Williams (1641-1650) had been Dean of Westminster, Bishop of Lincoln, and Lord Chancellor. In the first year of Charles's reign he had the seals taken from him, and was sent to the Tower. When Episcopacy was abolished, he returned to Wales, his native country, where it is said he joined the Roundheads, and changed his lawn for buff. He was buried at Llondegay Church.

Accepted Trewen (1660-1664) had been Bishop of Lichfield nominally since 1644. As his name shows, he was of Puritan family, but became chaplain to the king. His monument is in the choir.

Richard Sterne (1664-1683) had been Bishop of Carlisle. He was expelled from the mastership of Jesus College, and imprisoned by the Puritans. He had been chaplain to Laud, and was present at his death. His monument, unusually hideous, is at the east end of the cathedral.

John Dolben (1683-1686) was translated from Rochester. He died of the small-pox at Bishopthorpe. His tomb, also very ugly, is in the north side of the choir.

Thomas Lamplugh (1688-1691). The see of York remained vacant until the landing of William III. Lamplugh, then Bishop of Exeter, posted to London to carry the news of the invasion to the king and to assure him of his loyalty. James thereupon appointed him Archbishop of York. He quickly, however, gave allegiance to William, and was confirmed in his see. He assisted at William's coronation. His monument is in the choir.

John Sharp (1691-1714) had been Dean of Norwich and Canterbury. He wrote an account of the lives and acts of his predecessors, from Paulinus to Lamplugh. He was Anne's chief ecclesiastical adviser, a position he never abused. He died at Bath.

Sir William Danes (1713-1724). He had been chaplain in ordinary to William III., Prebend of Worcester, and in 1707 Bishop of Chester. He is said to have lost the bishopric of Lincoln by a bold sermon which offended Anne.

Lancelot Blackburne (1724-1743) was the subject of many slanderous stories, among others, that in his youth he had been chaplain on a pirate ship. He was certainly in the West Indies in his youth. He became Sub-dean of Exeter, and was forced to resign that office in 1702. In 1704 he was reinstated. He became Dean of Exeter in 1705, and Bishop in 1717. He is said to have been raised to the see of York for having married George I. to the Duchess of Munster. His manners were certainly free. Horace Walpole speaks of him as "the jolly old Archbishop of York, who had all the manners of a man of quality, though he had been a buccaneer, and was a clergyman. But he retained nothing of his first profession except his seraglio." He died in London, and was buried in St. Margaret's Church, Westminster.

Thomas Herring (1743-1747) was chaplain to the king. In 1732 he became Dean of Rochester, and in 1737 Bishop of Bangor. He was an ardent Whig, and when the '45 rebellion broke out raised £40,000 in defence of the Government, besides stirring up the people. For these good services he was translated to Canterbury. He died of dropsy in 1757.

Matthew Hutton (1747-1757) was also translated from Bangor; and from York to Canterbury. He died in 1758.

John Gilbert (1757-1761) became Dean of Exeter 1726, Bishop of Landaff 1740, and of Salisbury 1749.

Robert Hay Drummond (1761-1776) was the second son of Viscount Dapplin, afterwards Earl of Kinnoull. He was chaplain to George II., Bishop of St. Asaph in 1748, and of Salisbury in 1761.

William Markham (1777-1807) had been headmaster of Westminster School, Beatham. He became Dean of Rochester 1765, Dean of Christ Church 1767, and Bishop of Chester 1771. In the same year he became tutor to the Prince of Wales and Prince Frederick. He was buried in Westminster Abbey.

Edward Kruon Harcourt (1808-1847) was the youngest son of Lord Kruon. He became Bishop of Carlisle in 1791. He was a member of the Queen's Council during George III.'s incapacity, and one of the first members of the Ecclesiastical Commission (1835). During his primacy there were two fires in the minster, and he gave largely to the restoration fund. In 1838 he declined the renewal of the Harcourt peerage. He died at Bishopthorpe.

Thomas Musgrave (1847-1860) was the son of a Cambridge tailor. He was a Whig by politics, and in 1837 was appointed Dean of Bristol. In a few months he was preferred to the bishopric of Hereford. He is buried in Kensal Green cemetery.

Charles Thomas Langley (1860-1862), became headmaster of Harrow School in 1829, first Bishop of Ripon in 1836, and Bishop of Durham in 1856. He was translated from York to Canterbury in 1862. He supported the Liberal party in Parliament. He died in 1868 at Addington.

1863-1891—**William Thomson** (translated from Gloucester).

1891—**William Connor Magee** (translated from Peterboro').

1891—**William Dalrymple Maclagan** (translated from Lichfield).

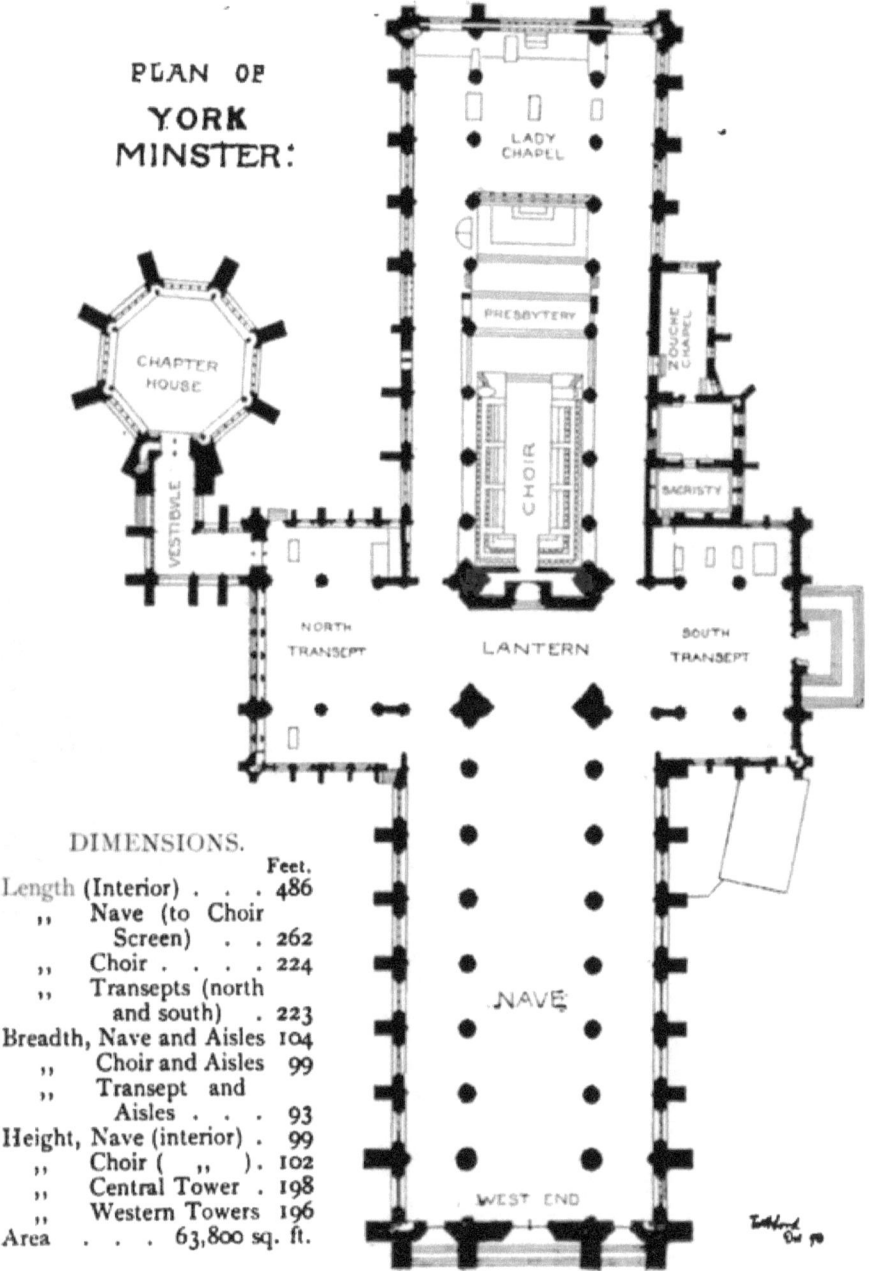

PLAN OF YORK MINSTER:

DIMENSIONS.

	Feet.
Length (Interior)	486
,, Nave (to Choir Screen)	262
,, Choir	224
,, Transepts (north and south)	223
Breadth, Nave and Aisles	104
,, Choir and Aisles	99
,, Transept and Aisles	93
Height, Nave (interior)	99
,, Choir (,,)	102
,, Central Tower	198
,, Western Towers	196
Area	63,800 sq. ft.

www.ingramcontent.com/pod-product-compliance
Lightning Source LLC
Chambersburg PA
CBHW022118160426
43197CB00009B/1076